NEW TESTAMENT EVANGELISM

How it is Practiced in Churches in Southeastern

Massachusetts and Rhode Island

Paul Lagasse

Library of Congress Control Number: 2017914424
Paul Lagasse, Rehoboth, MA

Lagasse, Paul. New Testament Evangelism: How it is Practiced in Southeastern
Massachusetts and Rhode Island.
Includes bibliographic reference.
Published by Paul Lagasse.
ISBN-13: 978-0-9964663-2-5

I affectionately inscribe this book to our Lord Jesus Christ,

in grateful appreciation of the fact that I now have eternal life

with Him.

Contents

Abbreviations

Comm.	Committee
Cor	Corinthians
Denom.	Denomination
IFB	Independent Fundamental Baptist
Math	Matthew
NT	New Testament
NH	Nursing Home
Rev	Revelation
RI	Rhode Island
Rom	Romans
SB	Southern Baptist
Tim	Timothy
UMCOR	United Methodist Convention on Relief

Tables

Figures

Preface

Having attended a non-denominational Bible-based church for nineteen years, I realized that there must be more to having faith in Jesus Christ than worshipping Him and sharing Christ with others at a personal level. After all, Jesus shared the Good News about Himself with not only those He knew personally, but with many He did not know from a human standpoint. He even taught His disciples to go out and share this news with others *they did not know* in Luke 10:1-2 (similar commandments regarding sharing the good news of Christ can be found in Matthew 24:14; Matthew 28:18-20; Acts 14:1-7; Acts 26:15-20; Acts 28:30-31; 1 Corinthians 9:16; Galatians 2:7; Ephesians 3:7-9; Ephesians 4:11-13; and 2 Timothy 4:5). If Jesus and His disciples could extend themselves to others they did not know, then so can I. In fact, in the aforementioned Bible verses, He commissions us to do so.

There is a great day coming when Jesus will return again. But for many it will be a day of gloom. Like in the days of Noah, people will be going about doing their business mindless about God, and then the door of the ark will shut. Where are the heralds in our generation? Who will share with the unaware stranger about sin, judgment, and Christ's sacrifice on the cross to save them from eternal hell?

You and I have been quickened by God's Word and His Spirit to share this news with others we do not know. This is why we are here (otherwise God could have transported us to heaven immediately after we accepted Him). It is the reason why Martha and Mary rushed from the resurrected tomb excitedly to tell the disciples that

Jesus arose from and conquered death! It is the reason why the angels sang Halleluiah

upon Christ's birth in Luke 2:14.

Let us remain true to His call.

Acknowledgements

I want to thank the faculty at Trinity Bible College and Theological Seminary for their support. Of special note is Dr. Elbert Elliott who offered his time and patience through the various milestones of the underlying dissertation for this book.

Finally, I want to especially thank my wife, Gloria, for her endearing love and support.

Introduction

Evangelism was a focal part both of Jesus' ministry as well as the disciples after Jesus' ascension with regards to the Church. God's perception of evangelism is that it falls under His calling and His grace. The proper perception of His calling is not from a human worldview, but rather from a divine viewpoint. Therefore, considering the orthodoxy of evangelism, the Church is required by Christ to incorporate evangelism into its ministry.

The biblical mandate refers to what Scripture tells us about evangelism when it comes to orthopraxis. It encompasses the daily beliefs and actions a believer should make to employ evangelism properly. The impetus for this is a sacrificial heart. A believer must hold onto the things of this world lightly so that obedience is preserved. The sacrificial heart of a believer brings a person into Christ's presence out of obedience, while having a disdain for those things which attempt to distract the believer from the Lord Jesus Christ and His Word.

The local church was destined to exist to be an evangelistic camp for the local community. Evangelism is an essential part of the local church. This is not based on a relative assessment of how we sort out Scripture amongst ecclesiastical activities, but rather it involves the power of God, and is therefore, a divine function with divine appointments. If the Church is to accomplish the mission of Jesus Christ today, then it must discover Christ's true mission according to His word. Christ's mission is not just to congregate in the four walls of a building, but to warn the local neighborhood regarding sin and its eternal consequences. The Church is accountable to share the gospel. Does the Church realize this?

This book was adapted from the author's dissertation as part of the requirements for the Doctor of Ministry degree with a major in Pastoral Ministry. The research question for the book is stated in Chapter 1 as: What are the similarities and differences between churches in Southeastern Massachusetts and Rhode Island and the evangelism as practiced in the New Testament by Jesus Christ, His disciples, and the apostle Paul, and how can churches in Southeastern Massachusetts and Rhode Island focus more on New Testament evangelism? This chapter deals with the guidelines and procedures to research this question.

Chapter 2 discusses the literary basis for the research question. First and foremost, what does God's Word say about this issue? This is necessary in order to adopt a divine viewpoint. We must stay tuned to God's perspective in order to arrive at a valid, Christian conclusion. Coupled with the exegesis is discussion from numerous authors on the subject. Their input was enlisted and prioritized based on the relativity of their discussion to the research question.

Chapter 3 sets the stage for the field portion of the research. It states the guidelines for initiating and performing interviews related to the research question.

Chapter 4 is a compilation of the findings based on the interviews. This compilation is viewed using various tables and figures to gain a better understanding of the results.

Finally in Chapter 5, the implications and applications are made regarding the research question. The eventual conclusion of this book rests on the orthopraxis of evangelism: what application can we make to our personal lives? It answers the question, "So what?"

Chapter 1

Research Concern

Introduction to the Research Question

The research question for this dissertation is: What are the similarities and differences between churches in Southeastern Massachusetts and Rhode Island and the evangelism as practiced in the New Testament by Jesus Christ, His disciples, and the apostle Paul, and how can churches in Southeastern Massachusetts and Rhode Island focus more on New Testament evangelism?

This author was surprised by a comment that a neighbor made about three years ago. Two of us from the church were performing door-to-door evangelism. After we asked our neighbor about his background and whether he attended church, he asked, "Why aren't other churches out here doing what you do?"

There are numerous New Testament references pertaining to both the importance and the practice of evangelism. It was a focal part both of Jesus' ministry as well as the disciples after Jesus' ascension. Thus, there is a place in God's Kingdom for evangelism. In addition, there are educational benefits promoting this research. It is the responsibility of each Christian, as well as the Church, to learn about evangelism and its importance in God's Kingdom and to make application from that learning.

Applied Research Purpose Statement

This research was performed to determine how effective Southeastern Massachusetts and Rhode Island churches are at practicing evangelism in their local areas. Are these churches practicing evangelism according to the way that Jesus Christ and His disciples practiced it? This research uncovered how these churches can be more focused on evangelism. This is important because the results of evangelism will, from God's point of view, determine whether or not people have a relationship with Jesus Christ and subsequently eternal life. There are eternal ramifications at stake here.

Delimitations of the Study

There are approximately 1,500 churches in Southeastern Massachusetts and Rhode Island as of this writing. This research did not cover those churches which are not Christian, since the New Testament rests on Christian principles. Even within the Christian realm, there are numerous denominations and this research is not intended to analyze all of them. An analysis of all denominations would be too exhaustive for this research, but could be continued as a further study beyond this research.

Credible participants were available for the following denominations: Southern Baptist, Independent Fundamental Baptist, Greek Orthodox, Methodist, and Non-denominational. Also, the research conducted within each of these denominations was not all inclusive for each denomination because there are numerous churches in the aforementioned area for each denomination. Thus, the analysis focused on a segment of each of the five denominations as an indicator of conformance to New Testament teachings on evangelism.

Furthermore, the portion of the research question dealing with how churches in this area can be more focused on evangelism did not result in a comprehensive list of improvements. Such a list may be too comprehensive for any dissertation or publication. The research of improvements for churches in this area entailed those improvements as deemed practical for this particular culture.

Hypotheses

Since the research was conducted in an empirical as well as a bibliographic fashion, the following hypotheses were considered:

1. Churches in Southeastern Massachusetts and Rhode Island are not following the biblical mandate for evangelism.
2. Most churches in Southeastern Massachusetts and Rhode Island do not understand the theology of New Testament evangelism.
3. The cultural setting for churches today in Southeastern Massachusetts and Rhode Island is vastly different than that of the Middle East 2000 years ago.

New Testament Evangelism

Terminology

authoritative word. God's Word as inspired by the Holy Spirit through men and recorded in what is commonly referred to as the Bible. It preempts all other considerations both in the spiritual and earthly realm. It is unalterable.

biblical mandate. The commissioning of men and women as directed by God's Word.

body of Christ. The set of worldwide believers in Jesus Christ. This set is composed of believers who have died, are still living, and are yet to live.

bridgers. That class of people born between 1977 and 1994.

cultural setting. The set of socioeconomic, philosophical, and religious traits of a local group of people.

denomination (Christian). A group of people that abide by the authoritative word in terms of beliefs, values, and sacraments.

eternal death. The eternal state of a person's soul as judged by God in Revelation 20 and 21, resulting in separation from Christ.

eternal life. The eternal state of a person's soul as judged by God in Revelation 20 and 21, resulting in life with Christ.

evangelism. The proclamation or telling of the fact that: (1) "all have sinned and fall short of the glory of God" (Romans 3:23), (2) "the wages of sin is eternal death" (Romans 6:23), and (3) "Christ also suffered once for sins, the righteous for the unrighteous, to bring you to God. He was put to death in the body but made alive by the Spirit" (1 Peter 3:18).

faith (Christian). Regarding the authoritative word, "confidence in what we hope for and assurance about what we do not see" (Hebrews 11:1).

repentance. Having remorse and sorrow over one's sin as a violation of God's Word, with a subsequent confession to Christ and the acknowledgement of His forgiveness as outlined in 1 John 1:9.

sin of adam. The violation of God's Word as described in Genesis 3:1-6, and the inheritance of the consequences of sin by each person subsequently born thereafter.

soul. The created portion of a person which exists in an ethereal form. It temporarily resides in a physical body, but exists in eternity in either heaven with Christ or in the lake of fire as described in Revelation 20 and 21.

techniques. Actions, ideas or events that can be used to employ one's belief.

theology. The study of God's point of view of both heaven and earth as communicated through His Word.

Procedural Overview

Research Question

What are the similarities and differences between churches in Southeastern Massachusetts and Rhode Island and the evangelism as practiced in the New Testament by Jesus Christ, His disciples, and the apostle Paul, and how can churches in

New Testament Evangelism

Southeastern Massachusetts and Rhode Island focus more on New Testament evangelism?

Building an Argument

These hypotheses support the research question:

1. Churches in Southeastern Massachusetts and Rhode Island are not following the biblical mandate for evangelism.

2. Most churches in Southeastern Massachusetts and Rhode Island do not understand the theology of New Testament evangelism.

3. The cultural setting for churches today in Southeastern Massachusetts and Rhode Island is vastly different than that of the Middle East 2000 years ago.

These hypotheses (or claims) were substantiated with reasons.[1] Evidence was then provided for each hypothesis. Consider when we have conversations with others. We make an assertion and then provide evidence for that assertion in order to convince others of our argument. When we are using qualitative methodology, the evidence is typically some type of behavior. The key question is whether or not the behavior noted is obvious enough to convince others of our claim.

This research also included informal interviews with human subjects. The responses provided by the interviewees were used to substantiate certain claims made by

---

[1] Kate L. Turabian, *A Manual for Writers of Research Papers, Theses, and Dissertations,* 8th ed. (Chicago, IL: The University of Chicago Press, 2013), 51.

this author. Since this research involved interviews with human subjects, it would normally be classified as a quantitative method since we collected data from several interviewees. However, this research also falls into the qualitative domain, since the evidence must be interpreted by others as being sufficient enough to substantiate the claims being made by this author.

If any objections or alternate views were noted by this author or one of the interviewees, the argument was then updated to include such items and the research was then conducted accordingly. This author also stated principles that make the reasons relevant to the claims.

Literature Review

Before the research was started, it was important to consider the biblical mandate for evangelism as exercised by Jesus Christ, His disciples, and the apostle Paul in the New Testament. An exegesis was then performed on Scripture passages related to this topic. One might ask, "Why wasn't this performed before the research question was developed?" It was important to first establish the research question and the bounds of that question before performing the exegesis. The exegesis was then necessary so that the readers could have a proper viewpoint during their critique. Are the claims being made by this author reasonable compared to what Scripture says? The results of the exegesis determined whether the claims need to be modified.

Bibliographic research was then conducted regarding the following topics:

1. What is the biblical mandate for evangelism as exercised by Jesus Christ, His disciples, and the apostle Paul in the New Testament?

2. What is the theology of New Testament evangelism?

3. What is the cultural setting for New Testament evangelism?

4. What techniques will allow Southeastern Massachusetts and Rhode Island churches to focus more on New Testament evangelism?

The sources for the research were from: (1) www.wordlcat.org (using the search topic "evangelism" under the Books tab, and (2) the ATLA Religion database under the EBSCO service in the Hunter Theological Library at Trinity Bible College and Theological Seminary (search topic, "evangelism"). Notes were taken on 4 x 6 inch flash cards using the template shown in Figure 1. The note cards were then organized per the Topic and then the Sub-Topic heading as noted in Figure 1. In Figure 1, the Sub-Topic headings contribute to the Topic Headings as discovered during the research.

The note cards were synthesized using the following techniques:[2]

- Compare various perspectives on the dissertation theme

- Identify general themes or topics that are common in the literature

- Identify apparent contradictory findings, noting possible explanations

---

[2] Paul D. Leedy and Jeanne Ellis Ormrod, *Practical Research: Planning and Design,* 9th ed. (Boston: Pearson, 2010), 79.

Theological presuppositions, as noted during the exegesis performed earlier, were critiqued with the topics from the note cards. These topics each formed a level of heading in Chapter 2 of the dissertation.

Discipline assumptions were then analyzed and critiqued objectively again using the note cards. These topics also formed a level of heading in Chapter 2 of the dissertation.

Author	Sub-Topic	Topic

Author's claim (*what is the author actually saying or how does the information contribute to the topic as it relates to the dissertation claim?*)

Author's evidence (*what proof does the author provide to substantiate the claim?*)

Figure 1. Format for bibliographic note card

Methodological Design

      This empirical research falls under the Qualitative method involving a phenomenological study.[3] This was conducted as lengthy, informal interviews (one to two hours in length) on a one-on-one basis.

Sample

      There are 648 churches in Rhode Island[4] and 857 churches in Southeastern Massachusetts as of this writing.[5] It would be a difficult endeavor timewise to interview a biblical leader from each one of these churches. Perhaps this could be considered as a further study. Furthermore, verbal consent would have to be obtained, and it is unknown as to how many of these leaders would actually consent to such an interview. This author has chosen to select biblical leaders which represent a cross-section of several denominations in Rhode Island and Southeastern Massachusetts. These leaders are respectable and deemed by this author as being honest and credible. This author has established a rapport with these leaders: one over the last year, one over twenty-five years, and the remainder over several years. This author has earned the mutual respect of these leaders. They represent the following denominations and locations, respectively: (1) Southern Baptist, Rhode Island; (2) Independent Fundamental Baptist, Southeastern

---

[3] Ibid., 141-142.

[4] "Yellow Pages," Yahoo, accessed February 18, 2016, http://www.yellowpages.com/providence-ri/churches.

[5] "Yellow Pages," Yahoo, accessed February 18, 2016, http://www.yellowpages.com/search?search_terms=churches&geo_location_terms=Rehoboth%2C+MA.

Massachusetts; (3) Greek Orthodox, Rhode Island; (4) Non-denominational (elder led), Massachusetts; and (5) Methodist, Rhode Island.

Data Collection

This author met with each interviewee separately, in a comfortable, relaxed, and fairly quiet setting. The questions listed in Appendix A (Interview Questions) were asked of each interviewee. This author made a separate file for each interviewee containing the list of questions, and recorded the interviewee's answers (Appendix B) into each file on his PC.

This author sought to subdue any preconceived notions regarding the subject matter. He kept an open mind, taking the perspective of the interviewee as the responses were gathered and recorded. The goal for each interview was to focus on what that particular interviewee was saying (irrespective of how the responses agree or disagree with this author's initial hypotheses).

Analysis of Findings

Compilation Protocol

The responses to the interview questions in Appendix B, as mentioned earlier, were stored in a separate file on a PC for each interviewee. The next step in the protocol was to generate an Excel file containing three questions in the first column and the number of denominations (maximum of five) responding in the affirmative in the second column (see Table 1). Secondly, a Word file was created by compiling all of the

New Testament Evangelism

denominational responses together for each interview question. This was then displayed later in the subsection below, Findings and Displays.

Findings and Displays

The denominational responses in Table 1 were then extrapolated into the graph in Figure 2. The answers to the interview questions are reflected in Table 2.

Table 1. Number of denominations responding to evangelism (format)

Question	Number of Denominations Responding in the Affirmative
Does your denomination hold to any specific views regarding evangelism?	[total number]
Does your denomination think that evangelism is important?	[total number]
Do you think that your immediate neighborhood is responsive to evangelism?	[total number]

Evaluation of the Research Design

An analysis was then made regarding the strengths and weaknesses of the methodology.

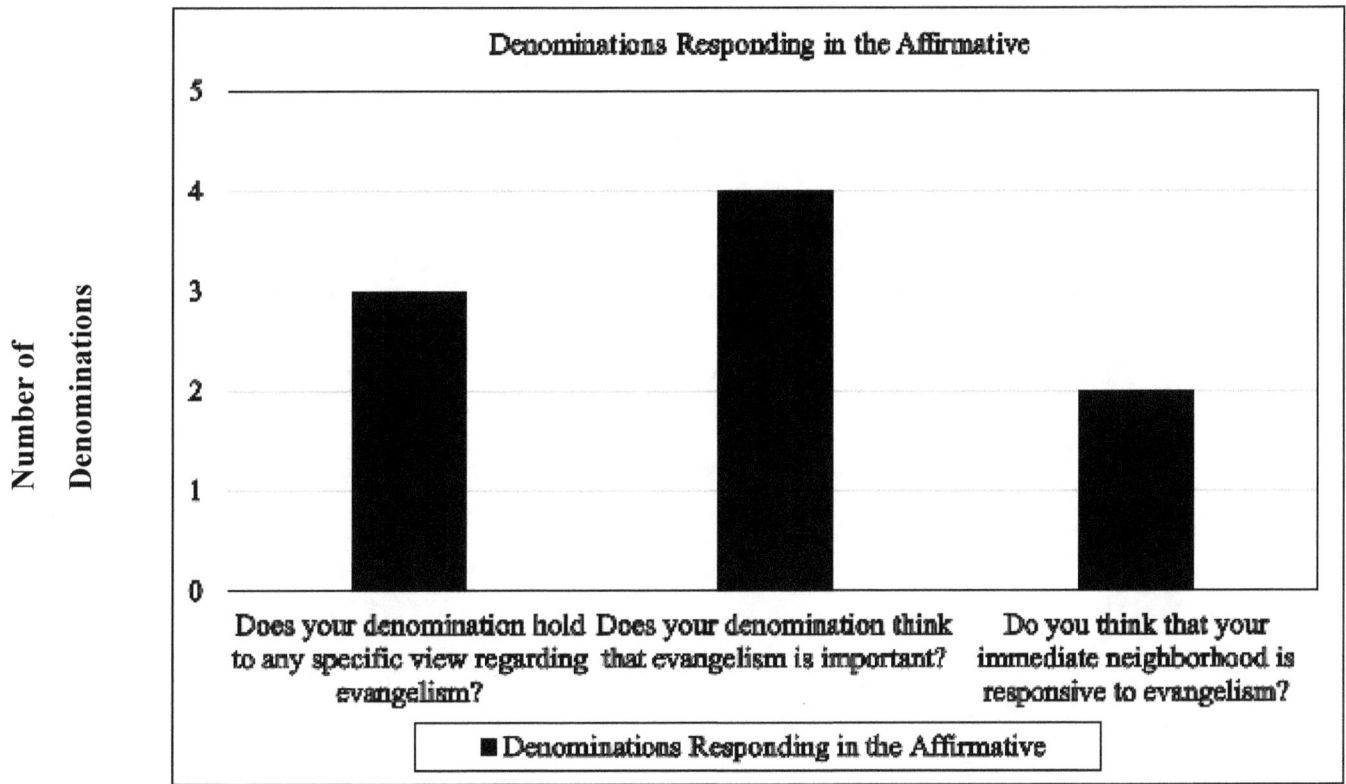

Figure 2. Denominations responding in the affirmative (example)

Table 2. Responses to interview questions (format)

Response	SB	IFB	Greek Orthodox	Methodist	Non-denominational
Definition of NT evangelism					
Techniques *you* deem appropriate for NT evangelism					
Specific views regarding evangelism					
Techniques your *denom.* deems appropriate for NT evangelism					
NT Scriptures applicable to NT evangelism					

New Testament Evangelism

Table 2. Responses to interview questions (format - continued)

Response	SB	IFB	Greek Orthodox	Methodist	Non-denominational
Techniques on evangelism as being applied in NT					
Immediate neighborhood responsive to evangelism (why/why not)					
Obstacles residents have to accepting Christ					
Obstacles fellow members have sharing Christ					
Church awareness regarding evangelism					

New Testament Evangelism

Conclusions

Applied Research Purpose Statement

This research was performed to determine how effective Southeastern Massachusetts and Rhode Island churches are at practicing evangelism in their local areas. Are these churches practicing evangelism according to the way that Jesus Christ and His disciples practiced it? This research also uncovered how these churches can be more focused on evangelism. This research is important because the results of evangelism will, from God's point of view, determine whether or not people have a relationship with Jesus Christ and subsequently eternal life. There are eternal ramifications at stake here.

Implications of Findings

How does the data impact the following hypotheses?

1. Churches in Southeastern Massachusetts and Rhode Island are not following the biblical mandate for evangelism.

2. Most churches in Southeastern Massachusetts and Rhode Island do not understand the theology of New Testament evangelism.

3. The cultural setting for churches today in Southeastern Massachusetts and Rhode Island is vastly different than that of the Middle East 2000 years ago.

These hypotheses were then discussed in light of the findings, and their effect on beliefs, theories, and practices.

New Testament Evangelism

Applications of Findings

      This author then developed subjective proposed outcomes as a result of the findings.

Further Study

      This entailed studies that can be conducted beyond the scope of this study. This is based on the findings or results of this study or as a continuation of the original scope of the study.

Research Assumptions

- The need for evangelism in Southeastern Massachusetts and Rhode Island will continue until the return of the Lord Jesus Christ.

- New Testament Scriptures such as the Great Commission in Matthew 28 are still valid and form the basis for local evangelism.

- God has preordained people with specific gifts to be in the area of evangelism (see Jeremiah 1:5 for preordination).

- The local churches in Southeastern Massachusetts and Rhode Island are part of the body of Christ known as the Church, and therefore, have a responsibility to participate in local evangelism.

- The act of evangelism is a divine act and cannot be accomplished without the influence of the Holy Spirit (see Luke 24:48).

Chapter 2

Literature Review

Before the research was started, it is important to consider the biblical mandate for evangelism as exercised by Jesus Christ, His disciples, and the apostle Paul in the New Testament. An exegesis was performed on Scripture passages related to this topic. One might ask, "Why wasn't this performed before the research question was developed?" It was important to first establish the research question and the bounds of that question before performing the exegesis. The exegesis was then necessary so that the readers could have a proper viewpoint during their critique. Are the claims being made by this author reasonable compared to what Scripture says? The results of the exegesis determined whether the claims need to be modified and formed the basis for the remainder of the research.

The second section of the Literature Review is entitled, Literary Presuppositions Regarding Evangelism. This section critiqued concepts provided by some theologians and biblical leaders. Since it is objective, it may present a world view different from what this author would consider.

Exegesis

The thrust of the exegesis was to answer the following questions which are reformatted from the hypotheses stated earlier:

1. What is the theology of NT evangelism?

2. What is the biblical mandate for NT evangelism?

3. What is the cultural setting for NT evangelism?

Therefore, this exegesis was not intended to be a thorough interpretation of Scripture based on the topic of evangelism. That task could be taken on as further study.

Theology of Evangelism

God's perception of evangelism is that it falls under His calling and His grace. The proper perception of His calling is not from a human worldview, but rather from a divine viewpoint. Isaiah records God's viewpoint in Isaiah 55:8: "For my thoughts are not your thoughts, neither are your ways my ways." We have to recognize that He is the One who initiates the calling, and not a biblical leader.

God's calling as it relates to evangelism.

Consider for a moment what God said in Jeremiah 1:5a, "Before I formed you in the womb I knew you, before you were born I set you apart." God is clearly the orchestrater of our gifts and talents. We are a product of how He constructed us. Therefore, there are those of us who are endowed with the gift of evangelism.

It would be appropriate for believers to consider themselves in the employ of Jesus Christ. God is not calling believers and endowing them with specific gifts just for the sake of empowering them. He has a well-orchestrated plan which includes all believers. The apostle Paul realized this and made it clear to the Galatians regarding his credentials: "Paul, an apostle – sent not from men nor by man, but by Jesus Christ and God the Father, who raised him from the dead" (Galatians 1:1). Believers should recognize their calling from God and not shy away from it.

God's plan in accomplishing evangelism. NT theology focuses the purpose of this gifting to build up and support the Church (or the body of Christ made up of all believers). Ephesians 4:11-13 further defines this:

> So Christ himself gave the apostles, the prophets, the evangelists, the pastors and teachers, to equip his people for works of service, so that the body of Christ may be built up until we all reach unity in the faith and in the knowledge of the Son of God and become mature, attaining to the whole measure of the fullness of Christ.

The word "evangelists" (*euangelistes*) means the "one who declares good news."[6] Again, we notice that the issuer of the gift is Christ. We must make certain that we respect the office of Christ when, as biblical leaders, we lead and encourage believers who have this gift. We are not promoting them as evangelists from our viewpoint, but from Christ's. A

---

[6] Spiros Zodhiates and Warren Baker, eds., *Hebrew-Greek Key Word Study Bible: Key Insights into God's Word* (Chattanooga, TN: AMG Publishers, 1996), 1628.

possible misnomer is that we leave the work of outreach to the evangelists, we leave the

work of shepherding to the pastors, and we leave the work of educating to the teachers.

This has the effect of a hierarchical church body, where there are a small group of people

that possess the aforementioned gifts, and the rest of the church body are not using any

gifts. The purpose of these offices, according to Wycliffe, is to train *others* to do the very

same work.[7] When an evangelist trains others to declare the good news, there is a strong

building up of the church body; likewise for pastors and teachers. God's plan is to call

and equip evangelists in such a manner.

From a holistic perspective, the Church is commissioned by Christ to proclaim the

gospel so that the complete number of Gentiles will enter the promise of eternity with

Christ. Paul proclaimed in Romans 11:25 that "Israel has experienced a hardening in part

until the full number of Gentiles has come in [to the Church]. "Full number" (*pleroma*) is

defined as "complete number."[8] That is, there is a specific quantity of believers that

Christ is bringing into His Church before He returns. Because God is omniscient, He

already foreknows and has foreordained those who will enter His Church.[9] The process

by which He brings souls into His Church is evangelism in accordance with the

empowering of the Holy Spirit. This is God's viewpoint for equipping believers to bring

other believers into His Church.

_____

[7] Charles F. Pfeiffer and Everett F. Harrison, eds., *The Wycliffe Bible Commentary* (Chicago, IL: Moody Press, 1962), 1311.

[8] Zodhiates and Baker, *Hebrew-Greek Key Word Study Bible*, 1663.

[9] Pfeiffer, *The Wycliffe Bible Commentary,* 1218.

God's enabling of believers for evangelism. As noted above from Ephesians 4:11, Christ gave some to be evangelists. This is a major construct in the confidence of those who share the good news of Jesus Christ, since the evangelist has the knowledge that Jesus Christ has ordained the proclamation of this news. This is what motivates a person to share, for instance, that they attended church last weekend when a co-worker asks, "What did you do last weekend?" It's what excites someone when they go out as a team to knock on doors to take a survey (www.ProclaimCourse.com) about how good residents think they are and then to share the good news of Christ.

The aspect that "Christ gave *some* [italics mine] to be evangelists" from Ephesians 4:11 infers that not all believers are responsible for proclaiming Christ. In contrast, Wycliffe purports an overlapping of offices between evangelists, pastors, and teachers in Ephesians 4:11.[10] When we notice other believers in the local church, each has a story about how they shared Christ with someone, or if not, their own life is a witness. We also notice believers shepherding other believers, and yet, the same believers are also teaching other believers. There is an overlapping of these three gifts among the believers in a local church.

Second, the offices given in Ephesians 4:11 are for the instruction of other believers in the church to learn how to serve in those particular areas. Therefore, evangelists are to train other believers how to share the gospel of Christ. Teachers have the responsibility to train others to be able to teach. Pastors have the responsibility to

_____

[10] Ibid., 1389.

train believers how to serve others in various capacities. This author recently observed a couple in the church who volunteered to provide clothing to a local shelter. They received donations from the local congregation for cold weather clothing. They also prepared coffee and donuts. Then they setup a table outside the shelter to distribute the clothing and food. At the same time, they also offered spiritual encouragement and guidance by talking with the residents and providing tracts. This opportunity was the result of training received through a Wednesday night Bible Study on the topic of evangelism. God does task biblical leaders to train others to do what they do.

God has confidence in believers whom He commissions with gifts to do His work. As noted previously from Jeremiah 1:5, God set us apart to do specific work that He formed us to do. The word "apart" (*qadas*) means "used for God's service."[11] Since He formed us to do this work, He then confides clearly in us. In Paul's letter to the Galatians, he mentioned that he was "entrusted with the task of preaching the gospel to the uncircumcised, just as Peter had been to the circumcised" (Galatians 2:7). The word "entrusted" (*pisteuo*) means to confide in.[12] As we proclaim the good news of Christ, we can have the assurance that God already confides in us.

In addition, God has enabled us to do His work through the power of the Holy Spirit within us: "you will receive power when the Holy Spirit comes on you; and you will be my witnesses in Jerusalem, and in all Judea and Samaria, and to the ends of the earth" (Acts 1:8). The presence of the Holy Spirit allows us to accomplish God's plan

---

[11] Zodhiates and Baker, *Hebrew-Greek Key Word Study Bible*, 1547.
[12] Ibid., 1662.

through us.[13] We can be confident that our actions and our words will be guided by the Spirit: "But when he, the Spirit of truth, comes, he will guide you into all the truth. He will not speak on his own; he will speak only what he hears, and he will tell you what is yet to come" (John 16:13). Therefore, each believer should recognize that they are equipped spiritually to serve the Lord. It is important that believers realize this. Otherwise, they may become susceptible to their own inhibitions, and worse yet, they might consider that they can do this work on their own strength. Paul was right when he encouraged the Philippians: "I can do all this through him who gives me strength" (Philippians 4:13). The phrase "gives me strength" (*endynamoo*) is defined as "to enable one to endure or handle something."[14]

God's grace as it relates to evangelism.

God issues grace as a divine instrument to produce a certain action in believers. The apostle Paul wrote to the Ephesians claiming that although he was the least of the Lord's people, grace was given to him "to preach to the Gentiles the boundless riches of Christ" (Ephesians 3:8). Paul's argument here is that he could not preach the gospel based on his own abilities. There was a necessary element that was required for him to preach, and that element was grace. Wycliffe claims that grace was not given for one's

---

[13] Paul Lagasse, *Understanding All About God: How to Obtain Eternal Life,* accessed February 29, 2016, http://understandingallaboutgod.com, 10-11.

[14] Zodhiates and Baker, *Hebrew-Greek Key Word Study Bible,* 1621.

enjoyment, but to pass something onto others.[15] Grace is a divine instrument used by God to motivate believers to act in a certain way.

Biblical Mandate for Evangelism

The biblical mandate refers to what Scripture tells us about evangelism. It encompasses the daily beliefs and actions a believer should take to employ evangelism properly. It order to be productive in God's eyes, a believer is one who "meditate[s] on his [God's] law day and night. That person is like a tree planted by streams of water, which yields its fruit in season and whose leaf does not wither – whatever they do prospers" (Psalm 1:2-3).

A believer's preparation for evangelism.

In order to prepare for evangelism, a believer must know Christ. Jesus Christ is the model for all believers, not only in terms of their faith, but also in terms of their actions. Believers typically become acquainted with Christ by reading, studying, and meditating on Scripture. In addition, a deeper acquaintance can be acquired according to Paul in his letter to the Philippians. Paul said that he wanted to know Christ in "the power of His resurrection and the participation in His sufferings" (Philippians 3:10).

Looking deeper into this verse, the word "power" (*dynamis*) means "essential power, true nature or reality of something."[16] Paul was not satisfied in just *doing*

---

[15] Pfeiffer, *The Wycliffe Bible Commentary,* 1308.

Christianity, he wanted to experience Christ in his own daily life. In particular, he wanted to live for Christ in the divine power that characterizes who Christ is. Therefore, Paul's viewpoint of his own lifestyle was not just a secular one, but rather a divine one inspired by Christ's power as Paul lived each day.

The other aspect of Philippians 3:10 refers to the sufferings that Christ endured. Here, "sufferings" (*pathema*) means "that the sufferings of a Christian are endurable because they suffered for the sake of Christ."[17] This infers a strength that is available, not from human means, but from a divine source – Jesus Christ. Wycliffe links "power" and "sufferings" together as part of the same experience of knowing Christ due to the single article in Greek: "being conformed [present participle] to his death."[18] Therefore, a believer's preparation for evangelism comes from a faith that rests in Christ's power as the believer trusts in Christ as difficulties arise. An example of this is when Paul and Silas were imprisoned in Philippi. The account in Acts 16:16-40 indicates that Paul and Silas were singing hymns while they were imprisoned. God miraculously freed them from their enslavement, but the fact that they were singing while under duress points to their trust in the power and sufferings of Christ.

A believer also prepares for evangelism out of obedience to Christ. Paul had this to say about his obedience as he wrote to the Philippians, "I consider everything a loss because of the surpassing worth of knowing Christ Jesus my Lord, for whose sake I have

---

[16] Zodhiates and Baker, *Hebrew-Greek Key Word Study Bible*, 1528.

[17] Ibid., 1657.

[18] Ibid., 1328.

lost all things. I consider them garbage, that I may gain Christ" (Philippians 3:8). Paul, here, is not distracted by those things which would interfere with his obedience to Christ. This is a key principle for the believer, since evangelism can only be accomplished through the aforementioned power and sufferings of Christ. Any distraction from the believer's obedience will compromise Christ's work through the believer. The impetus for this is a sacrificial heart. A believer must hold onto the things of this world lightly so that obedience is preserved. The sacrificial heart of a believer brings a person into Christ's presence out of obedience, while having a disdain for those things which attempt to distract the believer from the Lord Jesus Christ and His Word.

Believers also prepare for evangelism through determination, training, and perseverance. Paul attributes this preparation to that of preparing for a race, "I press on toward the goal to win the prize for which God has called me heavenward in Christ Jesus" (Philippians 3:14). The "prize" refers to the Olympic Games that were staged in Greek stadiums.[19] A judge would sit at a location marked with a square pillar known as the goal. He would have in his hand a prize which then inspired the runners to win the race. This would indicate that believers need to be focused as well as prepared. The work of evangelism requires training and commitment. It is a serious task. The end result for believers who faithfully practice evangelism is the heavenward "prize" that awaits them when they finish the race and meet the judge at the goal, Jesus Christ.

---

[19] James M. Freeman, *Manners and Customs of the Bible* (Plainfield, NJ: Logos International, 1972), 466-467.

How a believer engages with other believers regarding evangelism is important. The apostle Paul encouraged the Philippians to be "like-minded, one in spirit and of one mind" (Philippians 2:2). The word "like-minded" (*phroneo*) is defined as "to think of the same thing."[20] We notice from Scripture that the disciples and the apostle Paul traveled in pairs when proclaiming the gospel. There are obvious benefits to this in terms of mutual encouragement, but the directive being from Scripture imposes divine power when evangelizing in pairs or as part of a team. This concept is also true in other church disciplines such as pastoral care and education. A team or group of people who are of the same mind will work effectively when evangelizing.

Furthermore, Philippians 2:3b indicates "In humility value others above yourselves." The word "value" (*hegeomai*) is defined as to "consider."[21] How often do believers consider others on the team as well as those who are the object of evangelism? This type of consideration is self-less for the believer. It is not about how one feels, but rather how one can work with other believers and minister to non-believers. Wycliffe agrees with this analysis by indicating that valuing others is indicative of "thoughtful consideration . . . preferential treatment."[22]

---

[20] Zodhiates and Baker, *Hebrew-Greek Key Word Study Bible*, 1684.

[21] Ibid., 1630.

[22] Pfeiffer, *The Wycliffe Bible Commentary,* 1325.

A believer's action for evangelism.

      A believer seeks to do God's will. *How* does a believer do God's will rather than *what* is a believer doing to accomplish God's will? This is a characteristic of a believer that governs their approach to daily life. For example, when one gives of their time and funds for a particular service, do they do it with enthusiasm or with an apathetic heart? Paul indicated to the Corinthians that he was "compelled" to preach (1 Corinthians 9:16). This word means "out of necessity; opposite to willingness" (*ananke*).[23] Paul's viewpoint is that he did not have a choice. Since he was a slave to Christ, he had to preach. It was an inner conviction in his heart – something that would not go away, but would remain on his conscience. A few verses later in verse 19b, he said, "I have made myself a slave to everyone, to win as many as possible." The phrase "slave to everyone" (*douloo*) means "to be subject to."[24] This indicates a total commitment to the cause of Christ. The phrase "to win as many as possible" is not attributed to gaining as many converts as possible – that would be a human viewpoint, but rather to be completely subjected to the cause of winning souls for Christ. It is not what a believer wants to do, but what does *Christ* want to do through the believer.

      As Christians, we are working for the Lord over the course of our lives. The apostle Peter encouraged the Jewish believers to live the rest of their earthly lives for the will of God (1 Peter 4:2). The word "will" (*thelema*) is defined as "for God's own good

---

[23] Zodhiates and Baker, *Hebrew-Greek Key Word Study Bible*, 1584.

[24] Ibid., 1612.

pleasure."[25] This redirects the Christian's attention to view God's pleasure as the purpose for which they work. The human tendency is to view pursuits subjectively, but this tendency must be subdued so that God's pleasure is taken into consideration. The apostle Paul mentioned to the Corinthians that they are not their own – they "were bought at a price. Therefore, honor God with your bodies" (1 Corinthians 6:20). As we plan our work over the course of time, therefore, we should invest ourselves wholly to what God has called us to do in accordance with His word.

One may ask, "What is God's will according to His word?" Peter explained in 1 Peter 4:10 that the Jewish believers were to use their gifts to serve others. The word "serve" (*diakonia*) means "to care for someone's needs."[26] God is specifically saying that His will is to care for others. This is the position of humility, since it avoids self-will or self-pleasure and puts the emphasis on others. Interesting enough, those that require the most care tend to be those that have the most need. It's the reason why Jesus ministered to those at the hillside in Matthew 9:36 who were ostracized from society and in need of a shepherd. It's the reason why the twelve disciples in Acts 6 were providing food for the Jewish widows. God's pleasure is to care for those in need.

When some deviate from sound doctrine, be alert and continue the work. Paul warned Timothy, "For the time will come when people will not put up with sound doctrine. Instead, to suit their own desires, they will gather around them a great number

---

[25] Ibid., 1631.
[26] Ibid., 1606.

of teachers to say what their itching ears want to hear" (2 Timothy 4:3). Paul warned that there would be times when churches will deviate from the truth. His antidote for this was to "preach the word . . . [and to] correct, rebuke, and encourage" (verse 2). The importance for the true believer here is to deliver the fundamental message.[27] The true believer should be rooted in prayer and Scripture while delivering the message.

Paul further admonished Timothy to "keep your head in all situations" (verse 5). He was to be sober and alert, watching for those circumstances that would allow one to deviate from Scripture.[28] When times became difficult, Paul's advice was to "endure hardship" (verse 5). Certainly there would be times when following the right path would be difficult. We are in a spiritual battle against dark forces, and Paul wanted to encourage Timothy to remain steadfast. The word "endure" (*kakopatheo*) is defined as "to endure trouble."[29] The warning Paul gave was for all believers for all times.[30]

Finally, Paul told Timothy to "do the work of an evangelist" (verse 5). The word "evangelist" (*euangelistes*) means the "one who declares good news."[31] The key focus for a believer is to keep Christ at the forefront of our hearts, our minds, and our lips. We should be ready to give credit to God before someone else for everything He has

---

[27] Pfeiffer, *The Wycliffe Bible Commentary,* 1389.

[28] Ibid.

[29] Zodhiates and Baker, *Hebrew-Greek Key Word Study Bible*, 2084.

[30] For a recent example, see Erwin W. Lutzer's book, *Hitler's Cross,* (Chicago, IL: Moody Press, 1995). Lutzer mentioned the Confessing Church which was a group of clergy in Germany during World War II which stood up to not only the Third Reich, but also to the remaining German church which acquiesced to the unchristian teachings of the Third Reich.

[31] Zodhiates and Baker, *Hebrew-Greek Key Word Study Bible*, 1628.

provided. Paul concluded verse 5 by telling Timothy to "discharge all the duties of your ministry." The word "discharge" (*plerophoreo*) is defined as "to fully establish."[32] Timothy was to carry out the ministry fully. This was required not only to ensure that the good news was shared effectively, but also to keep him engaged in the truth.

The Cultural Setting for the New Testament

Jesus came from the Jewish tribe of Judah. Furthermore, he grew up in Nazareth and began His public ministry there (Matthew 1-3 and Mark 1). The foundation for the Jewish belief, therefore, was in the Torah (the first five books of the Old Testament). Jewish tradition was based on a divine relationship between Israel and Jehovah. God set forth this proclamation with the nation of Israel: "Now if you obey me fully and keep my covenant, then out of all nations you will be my treasured possession" (Exodus 19:5).

The setting for evangelism.

Jewish custom was based on laws set forth by God (as noted in Leviticus). Thus, the religious belief system was constrained to both a personal and national obedience to the laws set forth by God. Genesis 3, however, described how sin came into the world and the consequences of personal sin resulting in separation from God according to Isaiah 59:2 (temporary forgiveness and restitution with God was made only possible through animal sacrifices according to Leviticus 16). God proclaimed through the prophet Isaiah

---

[32] Ibid., 1663.

that Jesus Christ would make a final propitiation for sin and restore one's relationship

with Himself: "But he was pierced for our transgressions, he was crushed for our

iniquities; the punishment that brought us peace was on him, and by his wounds we are

healed" (Isaiah 53:5).

God prepares the setting for evangelism. Two thousand years ago, societal

communication was governed by local gatherings.[33] People shared thoughts and passed

along ideas while they met in groups. To gain shelter, it was common for the local Jewish

people to gather in synagogues. This afforded the disciples an opportunity to speak freely

about Christ. For example, Paul and Barnabas spoke effectively to a great number of

Jews and Greeks at Iconium in the Roman province of Galatia (Acts 14:1). Since this was

a localized gathering, they spoke boldly for Christ (verse 3). The word "boldly"

(*parresia*) means "freedom in speaking all that one thinks."[34] We note also from verse 3,

that God confirmed their message by enabling them to do miraculous signs and wonders.

Another consequence of being in a close-knit community is the fact that the disciples

were mistreated. Nevertheless, they still continued to preach about Christ in verses 5-7.[35]

---

[33] Freeman, *Manners and Customs of the Bible,* 335.

[34] Zodhiates and Baker, *Hebrew-Greek Key Word Study Bible*, 1660.

[35] For other types of settings, see John 4 for the conversation between Jesus and the Samaritan woman, and Acts 3 for the conversation between Peter and John and the beggar. These examples demonstrate other settings where God was at work in evangelism. Whether the physical setting was a mass group of people in a synagogue or two people talking by a well, God was and still is at work convicting hearts.

In addition, the tone with which one uses to share the gospel is also indicative of the setting. For instance, when Paul was in his house in Rome, he proclaimed the Kingdom of God with boldness and taught about the Lord without hindrance (Acts 28:30-31). We note here the same Greek word for boldness (*parresia*), indicated in the last paragraph. This describes that Paul had the freedom in speaking all that he thought. God puts the topics and thoughts into an evangelist's mind. So when an evangelist is speaking freely, they have the assurance that God is speaking to the other person's heart.

We must turn our attention to another Scripture regarding the topic of setting. In Matthew 28:19a, Jesus declared, "Go and make disciples of all nations." The word "nations" (*ethnos*) is defined as "those outside the covenant community."[36] The call here is to go outside the borders of the present gathering into the local community. That includes any ethnicities that may be represented in the local community. This is important, since spending time with these people will give them the opportunity of coming into a personal relationship with Jesus Christ.[37]

The proclamation here in verse 19 is to enlist people under the lordship of Jesus Christ.[38] Herein is the purpose of the setting. Christ's viewpoint of this proclamation falls under His plan to redeem His people, "For Christ also suffered once for sins, the righteous for the unrighteous, to bring you to God. He was put to death in the body but made alive in the Spirit" (1 Peter 3:18). This enlistment is to make followers of Christ,

---

[36] Zodhiates and Baker, *Hebrew-Greek Key Word Study Bible*, 1614.

[37] Lagasse, *Understanding All About God*, 14.

[38] Pfeiffer, *The Wycliffe Bible Commentary*, 985.

but more specifically it is to shape one's character. The word "disciples" (*matheteuo*) in

Matthew 28:19 is defined as "shaping of one's character and cultivation of worldview."[39]

The aspect of making disciples, therefore, is not only to share the gospel but to also help

shape one's character. We are now discovering that evangelism (as well as other gifts) is

not exclusively segregated to one function, but rather it encompasses other functions

within the Church. That is another reason why the gifts mentioned in Ephesians 4:11

(evangelists, pastors, teachers) are not meant to segregate people according to specific

gifts, but to realize that some people are more gifted in some areas that others, and yet,

they still have some gifting in the other areas. For instance, a person that is highly gifted

in evangelism may also possess the gift of providing pastoral care and the gift of

teaching. The point of Ephesians 4:11 (as well as the context of Scripture, especially in

light of Matthew 28:19), is to edify or build up the Church. God will provide the gifts He

deems necessary to each individual. It is not who has what gift, but rather, how the

Church is being built up.

    First generation believers did not have Christian presuppositions. The prophetic

message of Isaiah 53 had a two-fold purpose: (1) to set forth the prophecy that would

eventually be fulfilled by Jesus Christ in His restoration of broken relationships between

people and God, and (2) to prepare a foundation by which NT Jews and Gentiles would

put their faith and trust in Jesus Christ. Until this was realized in the first century A.D.,

---

[39] Zodhiates and Baker, *Hebrew-Greek Key Word Study Bible*, 1647.

both Jews and Gentiles did not have a Christian presupposition as a basis for their faith.

We note that in John 4:10-13, the Samaritan woman (being half Jew, half Gentile) did not

immediately recognize the opportunity of having faith in Christ. Jesus said to her, "If you

knew the gift of God and who it is that asks you for a drink, you would have asked him

and he would have given you living water." To this she replied, "Sir, you have nothing to

draw with and the well is deep. Where can you get this living water? Are you greater than

our father Jacob, who gave us the well and drank from it himself, as did also his sons and

his livestock?" Jesus then said, "Everyone who drinks this water will be thirsty again, but

whoever drinks the water I give them will never thirst. Indeed, the water I give them will

become in them a spring of water welling up to eternal life." Later in verse 25, the

woman said, "I know that Messiah (called Christ) is coming. When he comes, he will

explain everything to us." This points to the awareness of the prophecy by first century

Jews and Gentiles, but not the immediate realization of Christ's presence.

New believers were dependent on oral traditions. The formal method of

recording both religious and legal doctrines was the responsibility of the scribes.[40] This

was a specialized office, since the common layperson did not possess this skill. As such,

the teachings and work performed by Jesus Christ was propagated orally by the first

disciples. This method paved the way for home fellowships, where the disciples and other

---

[40] Freeman, *Manners and Customs of the Bible,* 341-342.

believers met regularly for teaching, fellowship, breaking of bread, and prayer (Acts 2:12-16).

The believer's response to evangelism.

Earlier in this exegesis, we covered God's calling and plan for evangelism as mentioned in Ephesians 4. The purpose of this calling and plan is to build up the Church. But how did this calling impact each believer at a personal level? Did Jesus Christ intend the practice of evangelism to be performed by a certain few or by all believers?

Let your light shine. Jesus spoke to the crowd on a mountainside in Matthew 5. He described them as the "light of the world" (Matthew 5:14). The metaphor for light comes from the Greek word, *phos*, which is a metaphor for the illumination shed forth by the indwelling of Christ in a believer.[41] Believers are to "illuminate a world in darkness because they possess Christ."[42] Note that this is an active use of the word "illuminate" rather than a passive one as in the previous sentence. Christ's intention, as He spoke to many people on the mountainside, was to have *all* believers *actively* sharing about Himself with others. It was not sufficient just to act nicely to others, because they may not know the reason for such good behavior. The purpose of specifically sharing about Christ was to give the credit or the glory for such illumination in a believer's life to Christ.

------

[41] Zodhiates and Baker, *Hebrew-Greek Key Word Study Bible*, 1685.

[42] Pfeiffer, *The Wycliffe Bible Commentary*, 937.

New Testament Evangelism

Philip shared Christ with the Ethiopian eunuch. The account of Philip sharing

Christ with an Ethiopian eunuch is given in Acts 8:26-35. What's interesting in this

account are the recorded references to God's leading in the account. Verse 26 tells us,

"Now an *angel of the Lord* said to Philip, 'Go south to the road – the desert road – that

goes down from Jerusalem to Gaza.'" Later, in verse 29, "The *Spirit* told Philip, 'Go to

that chariot and stay near it.'" Philip eventually shared the good news about Jesus in

verse 35. This account reminds us that opportunities for sharing Christ come from God

Himself. In John 15:5, Jesus stated, "Apart from me you can do nothing." The act of

evangelism, or sharing Christ, is a process where God is actively involved with not only

the recipient of the message, but also the believer presenting the message.

The local church's response to evangelism.

Earlier in this exegesis, we covered the importance of evangelism in the building

up of the local church as referenced in Ephesians 4:11. Was this an option for local

churches to include in their strategy or was it a requirement? How did the local church

actually implement evangelism in the first century?

The urgency to share Christ. We are reminded of that vivid picture when Christ

revealed Himself to John on the island of Patmos as recorded in Revelation 1-3. John was

so awestruck at Christ's appearance that he "fell at his feet as though dead" (Revelation

1:17). This appearance certainly got John's attention! If this was not a call to urgency,

then perhaps Jesus' claim in Revelation 1:18 that He "hold[s] the keys of death and

Hades" would certainly get a person's attention. Each of the seven churches in Revelation 2-3 were commended for their work, but were also rebuked for areas where they fell short in accomplishing Christ's work according to God's Word. The interface between Christ and the world was (and still is) through the Church. Colossians 1:24 provides us with the metaphor that Christ's body is the Church. Since Christ not only holds the keys to death and hades in Revelation 1:18 but also manages the book containing the names of those who will have eternal life (Revelation 20 and 21), it is therefore necessary for His Body (the Church) to share the good news of Christ with a world of recipients who are in danger of eternal death!

Sending out believers to share Christ. The account of Philip sharing Christ with an Ethiopian eunuch was given earlier in Acts 8:26-35. This is a personal way for Christ to work through individual believers. However, the account in Luke 10:1-24 describes the commissioning of seventy-two believers to go out into "every town and place where he [Jesus] was about to go" (verse 1). The main focus is not whether this is personal evangelism, door-to-door evangelism, or mass evangelism, but rather, the focus is on the "harvest" or need itself. In verse 2, Jesus explained that "The harvest is plentiful, but the workers are few. Ask the Lord of the harvest, therefore, to send out workers into his harvest field." Here we see the unique need of sharing Christ from God's point of view. Which point of view does the Church take today – Christ's or their own?

Evangelism versus the social gospel.

If evangelism is performed the way Jesus intended, we must come to the conclusion that it will result in social concern.

Jesus ministered to those ostracized from society. We can look no further than the model Jesus established in Matthew 9 when he ministered to those on the hillside who were ostracized from society. He had a concern for both their physical and their spiritual needs when He said, "The harvest is plentiful but the workers are few. Ask the Lord of the harvest, therefore, to send out more workers into His harvest field" (Matthew 9:37-38).

Jesus healed a blind man. We note from Mark 10:46-52, that the blind Bartimaeus called upon Jesus: "Jesus, Son of David, have mercy on me!" Jesus asked what He could do for him, and the man indicated that he wanted to see. Jesus healed him, and said to him, "Go, your faith has healed you."

Jesus healed a paralyzed man. How about the paralyzed man who was lowered in a stretcher from a roof because of the crowds. His determination and faith in Christ resulted in this statement from Jesus: "Friend, your sins are forgiven" (Luke 5:20). Jesus later instructed the paralyzed man in verse 24 to take his mat and go home. These examples demonstrate that social concern or social gospel is not void of evangelism, but works in tandem with it.

Literary Presuppositions Regarding Evangelism

These presuppositions were analyzed and critiqued objectively. They focus on perspectives from various authors – some having commonality and some appearing perhaps contradictory.

The thrust of these presuppositions was to answer the following questions:

1. What is the biblical mandate for NT evangelism?

2. What is the cultural setting for NT evangelism?

3. What techniques can be used to engage in NT evangelism?

Therefore, these presuppositions are not intended to be a thorough analysis and critique on evangelism. That task could be taken on as further study.

The Biblical Mandate for Evangelism

This section focuses on what Christian theologians view as the biblical mandate for evangelism. The categories of evangelism discussed are: (1) definition, (2) purpose, (3) audience, and (4) training. The previous section (Exegesis) discussed evangelism from God's viewpoint. This section will develop tangible concepts from Scripture that we can use from a human viewpoint as we begin to explore how evangelism works on a daily basis in the western culture.

The definition of evangelism.

We must first consider a number of definitions from various authors. George Hunter described evangelism as "the making of *new* [italics mine] disciples."[43] This certainly parallels the Great Commission in Matthew 28:19 ("Therefore go and make disciples . . ."), but it points to the fact that a person can only become a new disciple if they were first presented the gospel. This is embodied in the use of the word *new*. Hunter's definition of evangelism also specifies the making of a disciple. A disciple is simply a follower of Christ. When does a believer accomplish being a disciple? It is a life-long process. The New Testament disciples spent three years in the presence of Christ, but they were followers of Christ (i.e. obedient to His Word) the rest of their lives. Therefore, according to Hunter, evangelism is the result of a person receiving the gospel and then obeying God's Word for the rest of their lives.

Robert Coleman explained evangelism in this manner: "The good news is that God has acted to save a people for himself."[44] Here, the onus is on God. He works in conjunction with believers to present the gospel message to others, and then to convict them of their sin and change their lives to live in obedience to His Word.

---

[43] George G. Hunter III, *The Contagious Congregation: Frontiers on Evangelism and Church Growth* (Nashville, TN: Abingdon Press, 1979), 21.

[44] Robert E. Coleman, *The Master's Way of Personal Evangelism* (Wheaton, IL: Crossway Books, 1997), 10.

John Stott presented a shortened definition of evangelism. He defined it as "the announcement of the good news, irrespective of the results."[45] Stott's definition claimed that evangelism is the presentation of the gospel alone. It does not require a conversion experience (repentance and change of heart), nor does it expect a life-long process of obedience to God's Word. This is in stark contrast to Coleman who defined it also as a conversion experience, and Hunter, who added that it results in a life-long process. Certainly, Stott was providing room for the recipient's response. Not every person who listens to a gospel presentation has a conversion experience. Stott included this condition in his definition to allow both a conversion type of response on the part of the recipient, and a non-conversion response.

The definition provided by J.D. Douglas concurs with that provided by John Stott. Douglas claimed that "to evangelize is to spread the good news that Jesus Christ died for our sins and was raised from the dead according to the Scriptures, and that as the reigning Lord he now offers the forgiveness of sins and the liberating gift of the Spirit to all who repent and believe."[46] There is nothing mentioned here regarding the recipients response to the gospel message. It is simply a communication to the recipient(s).

Nevertheless, Edward Dayton and David Frasier offered a much more comprehensive definition. They claimed that "to evangelize is to communicate the gospel

---

[45] John Stott, *Christian Mission in the Modern World* (Downers Grove, IL: InterVarsity Press, 1975), 35.

[46] J.D. Douglas, ed., *Let the Earth Hear His Voice* (Minneapolis, MN: World Wide Publications, 1975), in *Planning Strategies for World Evangelization,* Edward R. Dayton and David A. Frazier (Grand Rapids, MI: William B. Eerdmans Publishing Company, 1990), 51.

in such a way that men and women have a valid opportunity to accept Jesus Christ as

Lord and Savior and become responsible members of the Church."[47] Their reference to

communicate the gospel can be understood as "offering knowledge."[48] This phrase agrees

with Stott and Douglas. However, Dayton and Frasier used the phrase *accept Jesus*

Christ, meaning "to change attitudes and lead to new behavior."[49] This goes beyond the

mere communication of the gospel and points to a conversion experience on the part of

the recipient. They went even further to describe *become responsible members of the*

Church as to "generate new relationships."[50] Still yet, Dayton and Frasier added that

evangelism also entails measuring results to determine if the strategy used is effective.[51]

This introduces a monitoring process which is outside of the scope of the communication

of the gospel and the conversion experience by the recipient. This goes even beyond

Hunter and Coleman's definitions, which described evangelism as a life-long process for

the recipient (i.e. to make disciples, per Matthew 28:19).

Ben Johnson offered a more over-arching definition of evangelism. His definition

puts the responsibility of evangelism on the local church: evangelism is "that particular

task of the church to communicate the good news of God's love to persons so that they

may understand the message, place their trust in Christ, become loyal members of his

---

[47] Edward R. Dayton and David A. Frazier, *Planning Strategies for World Evangelization* (Grand Rapids, MI: William B. Eerdmans Publishing Company, 1990), 52-53.

[48] Ibid.

[49] Ibid.

[50] Ibid.

[51] Ibid.

church, and fulfill his will as obedient disciples."[52] This definition takes evangelism to a new level. Up to know, we have considered several definitions of evangelism as a person-to-person or a person-to-many type of communication. Johnson's definition now adds the scope of a many-to-many type of communication. Was that the intention that Jesus Christ had in mind when He said "go and make disciples" in Matthew 28:19? Was Jesus addressing the *individual* believers or the *group* of believers (i.e. the Church)? Like Dayton and Frasier, Johnson offered a definition that includes a conversion experience and a life-long process of obedience to God's Word. This obedience, however, results in a replication of believers. If a recipient were to fall under this definition of evangelism, and thereby, become a believer in obedience to God's Word, they would recognize that Matthew 28:19 requires them to engage in evangelism. This is, in effect, a cyclical process of new believers coming to Christ.[53]

We must consider one final definition of evangelism called *saturation evangelism.*[54] This type of evangelism is an attempt to bring the spoken and written gospel to every person, across every strata, to every home and individual. Like Hunter and Stott, it seeks to disperse the information, irrespective of the response. However, the setting, or groups of recipients, now becomes all persons in the world. Perhaps this

---

[52] Ben Campbell Johnson, *Rethinking Evangelism* (Philadelphia, PA: The Westminster Press, 1987), 12.

[53] The basis for this is the fact that the New Testament Church grew after the Ascension of Christ to what the Church is today. It literally grew from three thousand (Acts 2) to millions of believers today (as well as many more who have since passed).

[54] G.A. Getz, review of *Saturation Evangelism,* George W. Peters, *Bibliotheca Sacra* 128 no 510 (April – June 1971): 153-154.

definition seeks to comply with the latter part of Matthew 28:19: "go and make disciples of *all nations* [italics mine]." This also defines the target audience for the gospel message as being all persons in the neighborhood of a local church, as well as foreign missions.

As mentioned earlier, George Hunter was an advocate of evangelism as being the formation of Christian disciples. To accomplish this, he described the following sequence:[55]

1. The believer seeks to "achieve a loving presence among them [recipients]"

2. The recipient receives the Holy Spirit approaching them

3. The recipient hears the gospel

4. The recipient makes a decision for Christ

However, Hunter lists four other approaches that he states may describe evangelism:[56]

1. The social gospel – the aspect of "let us help you" as promoted by Mother Theresa

2. Let God intervene in their lives to heal them ("let God help you") as promoted by Oral Roberts

3. Radio broadcast – let them "hear the Word" as promoted by J.I. Packer

---

[55] Hunter, *The Contagious Congregation*, 21-24.

[56] Ibid.

4. Crusade evangelism – let them "make a decision" as promoted by Billy

   Graham

Could it be possible that Hunter's sequence for becoming a Christian disciple could be

embodied into one or more of the approaches listed above? Is the work of the Holy Spirit

in developing a new Christian disciple limited to one particular approach or can it be a

conglomeration of a number of approaches?

In contrast, we can consider the work of John Wesley, a renowned evangelist in

the 18th century in the British Isles. He sought to help new converts in: (1) the

establishment of their faith, (2) attending class meetings, and (3) attending local

churches.[57] Wesley realized that the Great Commission in Matthew 28:19 ("go and make

disciples") involved more than just assisting another person in a personal conversion

experience with Christ. The phrase "make disciples" (*matheteuo*) is defined as "to train

as a follower."[58] Thus, he helped new converts in the building of their faith and

establishing them in a local church. Evangelism was not meant to be just a conversion

experience but a combined conversion and growth experience for a new believer. As

explained in the earlier section (Exegesis), the gifts noted in Ephesians 4:11 (evangelists,

pastors, and teachers) were not meant to be exclusive gifts, but rather, overlapping gifts.

For example, two people decide to knock on doors in the neighborhood to introduce

---

[57] William J. Abraham, *The Logic of Evangelism* (Grand Rapids, MI: William B. Eerdmans Publishing Company, 1989), 54.

[58] Spiros Zodhiates and Warren Baker, eds., *Hebrew-Greek Key Word Study Bible: Key Insights into God's Word* (Chattanooga, TN: AMG Publishers, 1996), 1647.

residents to Christ. When a resident has a conversion experience with Christ, would it be appropriate for one of the visitors to say: "Ok. That's great. You've accepted Christ. Have a nice day! Now let's move on." Is that what new life in Christ is all about? Certainly not! We would expect one of the visitors to inquire if the resident has children and then to explain about the children's program at church. In addition, the visitor may offer to pick up the resident and bring them to church. This was Wesley's point of view with regards to evangelism. Wesley had the gift of evangelism, but that gift was in relative proportion to the other gifts he had.

Evangelism is not an end to itself, but rather an extension of the church into the community. When a new believer comes to Christ, the church effectively has just extended herself into the community. William J. Abraham puts it this way:

> In the early church one could be relatively sure that the verbal proclamation of the gospel would be intimately linked to the Christian community and to other ministries of the church that are essential to the rebirth and growth of the new believer. For the early Christians it would be unthinkable to have evangelism without community and community without evangelism.[59]

In order to make this extension, believers therefore must use not only the gift of evangelism given to them, but also other gifts such as hospitality, teaching, and pastoral care.

-----

[59] Abraham, *The Logic of Evangelism,* 56-57.

The importance of evangelism.

Where is the place of evangelism in the local church? Is it a subjugated activity for those who "feel" impassioned or is it a direct responsibility of the church? James Logan claimed that "mission and evangelism have become compartmentalized rather than functioning as the central core of the church's identity."[60] Logan then proceeded to approach evangelism from God's point of view: "Where is the awareness of the biblical study of the God of grace who seeks and finds, and then in turn calls us to join in the divine venture of seeking and finding a world which in Jesus Christ God so loved?"[61] Logan introduced an interesting concept. Evangelism is a triangular process: God is at the helm (the redemptive Christ), we are the instruments of His grace poured out through us, and the recipients are those objects of His grace as they experience repentance. Therefore, we cannot view evangelism from just the believer's or recipient's point of view, but we must also include God.

To ascertain the importance of evangelism, we must consider several viewpoints. The first viewpoint is from William Abraham. According to Abraham, evangelism is a subordinate activity in the local church.[62] The primary goal, continues Abraham, is to worship God and bow down to Him in obedience, and to celebrate His majesty in one's

---

[60] James C. Logan, *Theology and Evangelism in the Wesleyan Heritage* (Nashville, TN: Abingdon Press, 1994), 11.

[61] Ibid.

[62] Abraham, *The Logic of Evangelism*, 182.

life.[63] Abraham is certainly entitled to this view, because Scripture does not prioritize the various gifts. Ephesians 4:11 lists the gifts of evangelism, pastoring, and teaching, but not in a prioritized order. The apostle Paul emphasized the importance of gifts to the extent that the Church reach unity, become mature, and attain "to the whole measure of the fullness of Christ" (Ephesians 4:13).

Billy Graham offered a much different viewpoint. The International Congress on World Evangelism met at the Palais de Beaulieu in Lausanne, Switzerland on July 16, 1974, at which Graham delivered the keynote address.[64] Graham stated that the primary mission of the Church is evangelism, leading to the ultimate goal which is the personal salvation of souls.[65] Other functions such as social action are important, but these are distinct and subordinate to evangelism.[66] This polarized view stands in contrast to Abraham, who subscribes to the worship of God as being most important. How can we reconcile both authors who have comparatively polarized views?

Let's consider another author, John Stott, who also spoke at the conference at Lausanne.[67] Stott considered evangelism as an essential part of the Church's mission, but it is not the primary mission.[68] In his lecture, Stott argued that the Great Commission

---

[63] Ibid.

[64] Billy Graham, "Why Lausanne" (keynote address, Palais de Beaulieu, Lausanne, Switzerland, July 16, 1974).

[65] Ibid.

[66] Ibid.

[67] John R.W. Stott, "The Nature of Biblical Evangelism" (lecture, Palais de Beaulieu, Lausanne, Switzerland, July 16, 1974).

[68] Ibid.

("Go and make disciples of all nations . . ." - Matthew 28:16-20) is distinct from the

Great Commandment ("Love the Lord your God . . ." – Matthew 22:37-39).[69] Hence,

Stott is more consistent with Abraham in recognizing that the primary mission of the

Church is to worship God.

A fourth viewpoint is provided by Michael Cassidy. His point is that evangelism,

social action, fellowship, teaching, and worship are all fundamental parts of the Church.[70]

Cassidy appears to be in league with Abraham and Stott, since Scripture does not

prioritize the various gifts as previously noted in Ephesians 4:11. The edification of the

Church (Ephesians 4:13) is what is most important, and not any particular gift or

function. To promote or highlight one gift above the others presents the danger of self-

sufficiency and pride, which would quickly quench the presence of the Holy Spirit. At

this point, it appears that Graham is the only one who attributes evangelism as the

primary mission of the Church, but we must consider that evangelism is Graham's

vocation. Is it true that one's vocation would elevate one gift or function above all others,

or is there a way to consider all gifts and functions as equally important?

Perhaps a fifth viewpoint from Ronald Sider might help here. Sider considered

evangelism and social action as being equally important but distinct.[71] He noted that

----

[69] Ibid.

[70] Michael Cassidy, "The Third Way," *International Review of Mission* 63 (1974): 17.

[71] Ronald J. Sider, "Evangelism, Salvation and Social Justice: Definitions and Interrelationships," *International Review of Mission* 64, no. 255 (July 1975): 251-257.

Jesus spent time and energy to heal the sick.[72] Why would he do so if they would be

condemned (i.e. not accept Christ)?[73] Since Christ considered preaching and healing as

equally important, maintains Sider, then evangelism and social action are equally

important.[74] This is consistent with all of the previous authors, except for Graham.

Perhaps Graham's viewpoint is that a person must first accept Christ before they can

experience any of the other gifts – and that may be his reason for placing a precedence on

evangelism.

This would be a good time to consider a sixth viewpoint from John Yoder. He

considered evangelism as being important for both society and individuals.[75] Yoder

thought that the groaning of creation for the Savior was an important criteria for the

mission of the Church: "For creation waits in eager expectation for the children of God to

be revealed" (Romans 8:19).[76] This is an excellent point. Yoder takes the position of

Christ and His bride, the Church. Isn't that the most important mission of God Himself –

the redemption of souls stained by sin through the shed blood and death of Jesus Christ?

Evangelism actually becomes an event whereby believers participate with Jesus Christ in

bringing lost souls to Himself. From this viewpoint, evangelism does appear to be the

most important gift or function of the Church – which concurs with Graham's viewpoint.

---

[72] Ibid.

[73] Ibid.

[74] Ibid.

[75] John Yoder, *The Politics of Jesus* (Grand Rapids, MI: William B. Eerdmans Publishing Company, 1972), 153-157.

[76] Ibid.

Therefore, the local church was destined to exist to be an evangelistic camp for

the local community. Consider this metaphor spoken by Jesus Christ: "You are the salt of

the earth. But if the salt loses its saltiness, how can it be make salty again? It is no longer

good for anything except to be thrown out and trampled underfoot" (Matthew 5:13).

Those are very strong words, but can the local church measure up to the words of Christ

and will she be obedient? Consider the saltiness (or lack thereof) in this quote from C.

Peter Wagner:[77]

> A growth problem is bound to arise when the outreach priorities are switched.
> This has nothing to do with other kinds of priorities, such as commitment to
> Christ and commitment to the Body of Christ, both of which I believe need to
> precede outreach. But if a church that is otherwise in good health allows
> nominality to dim its belief that people without God have no hope, either in this
> world or the world to come, and if the church does not act on this belief with
> aggressive evangelism . . . the church will enter a period of declining numerical
> growth.

Evangelism is an essential part of the local church. This is not based on a relative

assessment of how we sort out Scripture amongst ecclesiastical activities, but rather it

involves the power of God, and is therefore, a divine function with divine appointments.

Dayton and Frasier considered "that this message comes from God in the person of Jesus

Christ . . . This message is so important it has the power to convey the abundant life of

the Kingdom of God to those who welcome it."[78] We must establish the fact that Christ

prioritized evangelism over caring for people.[79] The noun form of evangelism is *gospel.*

---

[77] C. Peter Wagner, *Your Church Can be Healthy* (Nashville, TN: Abingdon Press, 1979), 117.

[78] Dayton and Frazier, *Planning Strategies for World Evangelization,* 49.

[79] Robert E. Coleman, *Evangelism in Perspective* (Harrisburg, PA: Christian Publications, Inc., 1975), 31-32.

This noun occurs more than 130 times in the New Testament.[80] Even though Christ cared for people and went out of His way to demonstrate His care (Matthew 4:23-24, Mark 1:21-27, Luke 4:31-36, John 1:5-14), His main focus was communicating the *gospel.* Perhaps this helps us to understand that evangelism rests with the broadcast of the *gospel* as opposed to discipleship. Both functions are critical to the Church, but discipleship cannot occur until evangelism has been accomplished.

Evangelism is crucial because God's main purpose is to restore a broken relationship caused by sin.[81] That is why He demonstrated His love in sending Jesus Christ into the world (John 3:16). A relationship needs to be reinstated before any succeeding activities can occur. Worshipping God based on the Greatest Commandment is most important for a believer, but becoming a believer must occur before God can be worshipped.

To enforce this point, God is looking to the local church to respond to the spiritual needs of the local community.[82] If the local church does not respond to this need, then which other organization will? God's nature is to work through the Church to warn the community about its evil ways in order to save their lives. Notice how God spoke to Israel through the prophet Ezekiel:

> Son of man, I have made you a watchman for the people of Israel; so hear the
> word I speak and give them warning from me. When I say to a wicked person,

---

[80] Ibid.

[81] C. Peter Wagner, *Strategies for Church Growth: Tools for Effective Mission and Evangelism* (Ventura, CA: Regal Books, 1987), 18.

[82] Abraham, *The Logic of Evangelism,* 180.

'You will surely die,' and you do not warn them or speak out to dissuade them from their evil ways in order to save their life, that wicked person will die for their sin, and I will hold you accountable for their blood. But if you do warn the wicked person and they do not turn from their wickedness or from their evil ways, they will die for their sin; but you will have saved yourself (Ezekiel 3:17-19).

In fact, God repeated the same warning in Ezekiel 33:7-9. If the Church is to accomplish the mission of Jesus Christ today, then it must discover Christ's true mission according to His word. Christ's mission is not just to congregate in the four walls of a building, but to warn the community regarding sin and eternal life. There is accountability for the Church to share the gospel according to Ezekiel. Does the Church realize this? According to Abraham, the Church has lost interest in spreading the gospel.[83]

The onus has to be placed on the local church to be responsible for evangelism. The only other human agent available is the community, and the community is not actively looking to Christ. George Hunter noted:

Most people in a community never know what a congregation has to offer or that it wants to share it, unless people from the congregation leave the church and enter the neighborhood to engage others in caring friendship and meaningful conversation and so open up the faith and life of the congregation as a live option to undiscipled people.[84]

The local church must reach out into the neighborhood in friendship and meaningful conversation.

In reaching out to the neighborhood, however, the goal of evangelism is not how many converts are won or what is the size of the church budget but rather "how many

---

[83] Ibid., 181.

[84] Hunter, *The Contagious Congregation*, 20.

Christians are actively winning souls and training them to win the multitudes."[85] This is a metamorphosis for the Church. It is a change in methodology as to how the leaders converse, encourage, and motivate their church members. The goal of the Church is that its believers carry themselves as *evangels* in the local community. This is the biblical mandate for evangelism.

As believers seek to minister to recipients, they should be mindful of the motivation behind sharing the gospel. There are two types of bondage that every recipient or unbeliever experiences: (1) inner bondage in areas such as lust, pride of life, drugs, alcohol, etc., and (2) the consequences of sin (eternal death).[86] It would be beneficial if the believer focused on the topic of God's redemptive love in restoring a broken relationship between the recipient and Himself. Nevertheless, the daunting fact that all unbelievers have immediate problems as well as eternal damnation cannot be minimized. This realization should be on the mind of the believer whenever they are ministering to others.

The focus should be on maximizing the spread of the gospel.[87] This should operate in parallel with maximizing the number of believers sharing the gospel. Therefore, various types of media should be explored (e.g. radio, TV, internet, newspapers) in addition to various events (e.g. children's summer program, Chamber of Commerce events for the family, car washes, block parties). The goal is not to maximize

---

[85] Robert E. Coleman, *The Master Plan of Evangelism* (Grand Rapids, MI: Fleming H. Revell, 1993), 103.

[86] Alan Walker, *The New Evangelism* (Nashville, TN: Abingdon Press, 1975), 13.

[87] John Finney, *Emerging Evangelism* (London: Darton, Longman and Todd Ltd, 2004), 26.

the number of conversions, but rather, to maximize the number of ways to spread the gospel.

The audience for evangelism.

The geographical scope of evangelism is everywhere.[88] Therefore, there is no limitation as to where the gospel can be spread; this could be the local neighborhood, the city, the country, as well as other countries. Jesus was specific about this when He said, "But you will receive power when the Holy Spirit comes on you; and you will be my witnesses in Jerusalem, and in all Judea and Samaria, and to the ends of the earth" (Acts 1:8). This is coupled with the strata within a local community. Businesses as well as residents should be contacted.[89] The two types of people available in a local community are the people who live there and the people who work there.

But if the Church is made up of *evangels*, one must then consider who the audience is. Who are the recipients of the gospel of Christ? The spiritual nature of people reflect a wide diversity of beliefs. People who consider themselves "religious" may believe in any number of faiths. In addition, there are those who would not consider themselves religious, but they too, may subscribe to any particular faith. This is an important principle for the *evangels,* since they must know who they are addressing.

---

[88] Sterling W. Huston, *Crusade Evangelism and the Local Church* (Minneapolis, MN: World Wide Publications, 1984), 35.

[89] C.E. Autrey, *Evangelism in the Acts* (Grand Rapids, MI: Zondervan, 1964), 82.

For example, Paul addressed cultured pagans in the Grecian city of Athens - a

province in Achaia.[90] As he met with the spiritual leaders who were polytheists, he

addressed them by saying,

> People of Athens! I see that in every way you are very religious. For as I walked
> around and looked carefully at your objects of worship, I even found an altar with
> this inscription: TO AN UNKOWN GOD. So you are ignorant of the very thing
> you worship – and this is what I am going to proclaim to you (Acts 17:22-23).

The audience was religious, yet they were not knowledgeable about the Torah. This

presented a different audience for Paul.[91] *Evangels* will meet those who consider

themselves religious. The key point for the *evangel* is to be prepared to segue into a

conversation about Christ. Paul's point of view was to place himself in their position, and

approach the gospel message of Christ from their viewpoint. That is why Paul spoke to

those in Corinth in this fashion: "I have become all things to all people so that by all

possible means I might save some" (1 Corinthians 9:22).

In another setting, Paul and Barnabas were in the city of Lystra in the province of

Galatia (Acts 14:8-18). Paul healed a man that was lame. When the crowd saw this they

shouted, "The gods have come down to us in human form!" These people were immersed

in a culture which ascribed to Greek gods in a Roman world. They were uncultured

pagans.[92] The crowd thought that Paul and Barnabas were gods and attempted to offer

sacrifices to them. Paul segued with these words, "Friends, why are you doing this? We

---

[90] Jerram Barrs, *The Heart of Evangelism* (Wheaton, IL: Crossway Books, 2011), 184.

[91] Ibid.

[92] Ibid.

too are only human, like you. We are bringing you good news, telling you to turn from these worthless things to the living God, who made the heavens and the earth and sea and everything in them." *Evangels* must be ready to give glory to Jesus Christ and not to themselves.

We must also consider the generational aspect of the audience. For example, in a survey recorded in USA Today College, about 70% of the Boomers believe in God, but only about 50% of the Millennials have this belief.[93] However, we notice not just a downtrend from one generation to the next, but also within the same generation. In 2010, 74% of the Millennials responded positively to religious institutions. This number dropped to 55% in 2016.[94] The Millennial generation are the young workers of today and the influencers of tomorrow, yet their spiritual tendencies are drifting away from God. This generation, too, represents the audience that believers are to evangelize.

A believer must recognize that the culture of today is materialistic and is not inherently receptive to the gospel of Christ. Marva Dawn observed that our society "worships money, power, efficiency, immediacy, and control" whereas the Christian culture is "generous, meek (in the biblical sense), reflective, eternally minded, and obedient."[95] The focus of evangelism is the battle for the soul of a recipient. Those who

---

[93] Kristen Rein, *USA College Today,* last modified January 5, 2016, accessed March 14, 2016, http://college.usatoday.com/2016/01/05/survey-millenials-views-of-religion-news-media-grows-increasingly-negative.

[94] Ibid.

[95] Marva J. Dawn, *Reaching Out without Dumbing Down: A Theology of Worship for this Urgent Time* (Grand Rapids, MI: Eerdmans Publishing Company, 1995).

New Testament Evangelism

do not know Christ are engulfed in a vacuum of sin and may not even realize that are

despondent and separated from God.

Training for evangelism.

The biblical mandate for training comes from Christ: "Follow me and I will make

you fishers of men" (Mark 1:17). D. James Kennedy issued the question, "Who will do

this?"[96] Jesus provided the answer in Acts 1:8, "*you* [italics mine] will be my witnesses."

Jesus referred to the Church as being those who would be His witnesses. Therefore, it is

not appropriate for believers to point fingers at someone else when it comes to

evangelism, but each believer should consider their role to evangelize with respect to the

measure of the gift given them, their circle of influence, and the empowering of the Holy

Spirit (Acts 1:8).

The empowering of the Holy Spirit is essential to evangelism, but the union

between the Spirit and the believer is embodied in prayer. E.M. Bounds claimed that:[97]

> The real sermon is made in the closet. The man – God's man – is made in the
> closet. His life and his most profound convictions are born in his secret
> communion with God. The burdened and tearful agony of his spirit, his weightiest
> and sweetest messages are received when alone with God. Prayer makes the man;
> prayer makes the preacher; prayer makes the pastor.

Even though this quote focused on the sermon, it is applicable to any activity in a

believer's life. As Bounds referred to above, the messages and convictions of God are

---

[96] D. James Kennedy, *Evangelism Explosion* (London: Coverdale House Publishers, 1970), 2.

[97] E.M. Bounds, *Power Through Prayer* (Springdale, PA: Whitaker House, 1982), 13.

manifested in the believer during prayer. Thus, prayer is a critical component both in training for evangelism as well as the practice thereof.

If prayer is the foundation for any activity including evangelism, a believer must root out pride. There must be an emptiness or humility in a believer's heart if the Holy Spirit is to fill the heart with His plan. In fact, pride can prevent a believer as well as the local church from becoming effective in evangelism. Proverbs 3:10 says that "Pride leads to conflict" (Proverbs 13:10). 1 Corinthians 13:4 reminds us that "Love is patient, love is kind. It does not envy, it does not boast, it is not *proud* [italics mine]. It does not dishonor others, it is not *self-seeking* [italics mine]." David Roper dissociated pride into its root causes: "Quarrels are fueled by pride, by needing to be right, by wanting our way, or by defending our turf or egos."[98] These causes are itemized below for clarity:

1. Needing to be right

2. Wanting our way

3. Defending our turf

4. Defending our ego

As believers, we need to rid ourselves of these concerns. We cannot harbor them and be filled with the Spirit at the same time to be effective for God's Kingdom work. Here are Roper's suggestions for humility, which should be part of the training for evangelism:[99]

---

[98] David Roper, "The Two Bears," *Our Daily Bread* 60, no. 8 (August 2015): 12.
[99] Ibid.

New Testament Evangelism

1. Set aside our selfish ambition

2. Acknowledge the limits of our understanding

3. Listen to the other person's point of view

4. Allow our ideas to be corrected

These are very strong concerns to overcome. Yet, each believer must be trained to incorporate these values into their life.

When it comes to ambition, believers should recognize that Christian authority operates as a function, not status.[100] As a person trains and grows in faith, it is inevitable that the question of authority will arise. Jesus addressed this with the following:

> You know that the rulers of the Gentiles lord it over them, and their high officials exercise authority over them. Not so with you. Instead, whoever wants to become great among you must be your servant, and whoever wants to be first must be your slave – just as the Son of Man did not come to be served, but to serve, and to give his life as a ransom for many (Matthew 20:25-28).

This requires the believer to have a proper frame of mind when ministering. A believer must search their heart on a regular basis to ascertain if they are ministering with a pure motive. Regular times of prayer, reflection, and reading God's Word should help with this. Table 3 provides guidance when checking our hearts for a right motive.

Once believers are trained to conduct their lives in humility, they must be trained to love God and their neighbors (both believers and unbelievers). Homer Lindsey, pastor of First Baptist Church of Jacksonville, Florida, urged his members to evangelize but to

---

[100] Gaines Dobbins, *Evangelism According to Christ* (Nashville, TN: Broadman, 1949), 127-128.

Table 3. A contrast of self-righteous versus true service[101]

Self-Righteous Service	True Service
Human effort	Divine effort
Expending huge amounts of energy	Minimal human energy
Impressed with impressive gains	Drawn to small service
Requires external rewards	Content to be hidden
Highly concerned about results	No need to calculate results
Chooses whom to serve	Indiscriminate in ministry
Affected by moods	Ministers because there is a need
Insensitive	Listen with patience and understanding before acting
Fractures community	Builds community

no avail.[102] He then resolved to preach on the Great Commandments to love God and your neighbor. His sermon was prepared from Matthew 22:36-40, where one of the Pharisees and Sadducees asked Jesus, "Teacher, which is the greatest commandment in the Law?" Jesus replied, "Love the Lord your God with all your heart and with all your soul and with all your mind. This is the first and greatest commandment. And the second

---

[101] Ibid., 128.

[102] Roy J. Fish and J.B. Conant, *Every Member Evangelism for Today* (New York, NY: Harper and Row Publishers, 1922), 43.

is like it: Love your neighbor as yourself. All the Law and the Prophets hang on these two

commandments." After Lindsey preached on this for a while, scores of members were

winning hundreds of unbelievers to Christ every year.[103]

This Scripture and this story gives credence to the commandment to Love God

and our neighbors as the primary commandment. Evangelism (also known as the Great

Commission in Matthew 28) would then be a subordinate activity to the primary

commandment as noted earlier by Abraham. The story from Lindsey indicates that there

is a praxis involving the Great Commandments (Matthew 22) and the Great Commission

(Matthew 28). The Great Commandments must be applied first in ministry before the

Great Commission can be applied. This is not just a theological sequence, but rather it

describes the work of the Holy Spirit in concert with God's Word in bringing the gospel

to unbelievers. If we are looking for a process that works, then we should consider

Lindsey's biblical method of preaching on the Great Commandments first, and then the

Great Commission second.

But in order to comply with the Great Commission, Pastors (as leaders) are

responsible for motivating their congregations to evangelize.[104] Someone has to take the

responsibility for performing this function, and if the pastors don't, who will? Pastors act

as models for shaping the culture of their congregations. How is the culture of their

congregations shaped? Are they more concerned about church programs than lost souls?

---

[103] Ibid.

[104] Donald A. McGavran, *Effective Evangelism: A Theological Mandate* (Phillipsburg, NJ: Presbyterian & Reformed Publishing Company, 1988), 154.

What would Jesus think of our pastors as models? Donald McGavran had this to say

about a pastor's responsibility to motivate their congregation to evangelize:[105]

> Some pastors have special gifts in evangelism. Many do not. But all pastors have
> the responsibility to facilitate evangelism in and through their congregations.
> Pastoral leadership in evangelism extends from the pulpit and classroom to the
> people in the pew who are moved to action by the Word and the Spirit and
> encouraged by the pastor's interest and example.

This type of leadership from the pulpit and the classroom extends into the

personal lives and behaviors of pastors. Pastors are the models for their congregations.

Calvin Ratz observed that "It's been said, 'a student learns what his teacher knows, but a

disciple becomes what his master is.' My people will not become what I say they should

be; they'll become what they see is important in my life. And that's true with

evangelism."[106] This is a striking comment, since pastors preach weekly to their

congregations about how to apply Scripture to one's personal life. Do members act on

what the pastor preaches, or do they model their lives after what they perceive is the

lifestyle of their pastor? Certainly people will listen to sermons, but at the same time,

they are observing how the pastor lives and what they consider important. How pastors

prioritize their lives will certainly impact how the members prioritize their lives.

Pastors do set an example and should have a positive attitude when reaching out

to the unchurched. Eventually, reaching out to those outside the church will result in

growth inside the church. Most pastors, however, desire growth if it does not affect the

---

[105] Ibid.

[106] Calvin Ratz, Frank Tillapaugh, and Myron Ausburger, *Mastering Outreach & Evangelism* (Portland, OR: Multnomah, 1990), 26.

status quo of the church.[107] Ben Johnson noted that "resistance to a change of style and composition and a refusal to share power block sustained growth."[108] This is not a straight-forward manner, but pastors must accept dynamic changes within the leadership and within the culture of the congregation. This will likely include sharing power. It is a humbling experience for a pastor to accept this. It might be worthwhile for the pastor to pray and reflect on 1 Corinthians 13:4: "Love . . . does not envy . . . it is not proud."

When it comes to training for evangelism, pastors need a proper perspective. They should be training members to evangelize rather than evangelizing themselves.[109] Roy Fish and J.E. Conant stated that even evangelists should not be the only ones doing the work: "An evangelist is not to go to a field and reap the harvest for the church while they [fellow believers] look on. He is to lead, instruct, and direct the harvesters as they go out into the field and gather in the harvest themselves."[110] Unfortunately, the statistics do not indicate that pastors are training their members. Only 3-4% of pastors take their members out to evangelize and only 1½% of the members in a church body actually evangelize themselves.[111] D. James Kennedy points to Acts 8 as the presupposition for why pastors should train their members.[112] After the stoning of Stephen, Luke indicated that "A great persecution broke out against the church in Jerusalem, and *all except the apostles* were

---

[107] Ben Johnson, *Evangelism Primer* (Atlanta, GA: John Knox Press, 1983), 70.

[108] Ibid.

[109] Kennedy, *Evangelism Explosion,* 6.

[110] Fish and Conant, *Every Member Evangelism for Today,* 16.

[111] Kennedy, *Evangelism Explosion,* 7.

[112] Ibid., 6.

scattered throughout Judea and Samaria" (Acts 8:1). The reference, "all except the apostles," refers to the believers rather than the apostles, or what we might consider today as the original pastors after Christ. Acts 8:4 then follows with, "Those who had been scattered preached the word wherever they went." One definition of a disciple is not just an unbeliever coming to Christ, but a believer who is trained to spread the gospel so that an unbeliever can also come to Christ. This is a spiritual replication that defines what Jesus commanded in Matthew 28:19, when He said, "go and make disciples."

Michael Green provided a solid approach to help pastors mobilize their congregations for evangelism:[113]

1. Gain a passion for evangelism

2. Teach about it

3. Model it

4. Revive worship

5. Build up a team of committed volunteers

6. Generate unity within the team and the staff

7. Teach about spiritual weapons – prayer, Word, Holy Spirit, holiness, love

---

[113] Michael Green, *Evangelism through the Local Church* (Nashville, TN: Thomas Nelson Publishers, 1990), 414-415.

New Testament Evangelism

Green's approach is a structured, well-thought plan to promoting evangelism within the local church. Evangelism is not just recruiting a few volunteers and then proceed to visit households, but rather, it is a well-conceived, prayerful process. Cultivating a passion within the congregation takes time. In fact, it is very similar to the process of sanctification in a believer. In sanctification, believers grow in faith over a period of time by subjecting themselves to a number of opportunities: personal prayer and study of God's Word, teaching (*didache*), preaching (kerygma), fellowship (*koinonia*), and service (*diaconia*). Green's seven-step process is intended to "groom" volunteers over time to engage in evangelism.

In order for a believer to evangelize or to become an effective witness for Christ, they must have a Christian character. This type of character must adhere to God's Word, but Poh Fang Chia describes these biblical characters as defining a good witness:[114]

1. Eager to do good (1 Peter 3:13)

2. Live obediently in Christ

3. Have a good conscience

4. Be prepared to explain to others why we have such a hope (1 Peter 3:15)

This should be coupled with the attitude of offering a gently response when people attack us for our faith. We must realize that "Christ provides us with grace to reach even those who don't agree with us."[115]

---

[114] Poh Fang Chia, "Gentle Lights," *Our Daily Bread* 60, no. 8, 10.

If evangelism is to grow, it must involve a recruiting program. George Hunter referenced Rick Warren's model at Saddleback Valley Community Church.[116] This model seeks to find out how believers are gifted with respect to evangelism. Do they have compassion for the lost? Are they willing to take the initiative to present the gospel through various venues? Once it is determined how these people are gifted, then they are placed in ministry. This infers delegation if pastors are to expect their members to serve in the capacity that God has called them.

The biblical mandate for training resides with a "concentrated few."[117] This was certainly Jesus' model when he reiterated this with the Father:

> I have revealed you to those whom you gave me out of the world. They were yours; you gave them to me and they have obeyed your word. Now they know that everything you have given me comes from you. For I gave them the words you gave me and they accepted them. They knew with certainty that I came from you, and they believed that you sent me. I pray for them, I am not praying for the world, but for those you have given me, for they are yours (John 17:6-9).

We note from the New Testament that Jesus focused on the twelve disciples regarding training. If He wanted to, He could have trained many more people. The limitation was not on His end, but rather on the disciples end. We have to consider the size of the group of the twelve disciples whenever they met. Not only did they have a certain amount of space in the room of a house whenever they met, but each disciple required some

---

[115] Ibid.

[116] George G. Hunter III, "The Apostolic Identity of the Church and Wesleyan Christianity," in *Theology and Evangelism in the Wesleyan Heritage*, ed. James C. Logan (Nashville, TN: Abingdon Press, 1994), 169.

[117] Coleman, *The Master Plan of Evangelism,* 29-31.

personal time with Jesus. Jesus' ministry involving His disciples lasted only about three

years, and that was a limiting factor when attempting to spend one-on-one time with each

disciple in addition to the other tasks that Jesus performed. We note similar examples

from Paul when he mentored Timothy (1 Timothy 1:1-2) and Titus (Titus 1:1-4). Thus,

the more concentrated the group, the more effective the instruction.[118] In fact, D. James

Kennedy claimed that it is more important to train one member for evangelism than to

win one unbeliever to Christ.[119] The reason for this stems from the multiplication

principle using a binary tree. If the pastor trains two believers to evangelize, then it is

expected that these believers will be capable of each training two more members. This

would result in an exponential growth of gifted evangelists. This type of growth is not

only critical for the local church, but also for the Kingdom of Christ.

This does not exclude the responsibility of all believers to evangelize. Jesus

declared this when He taught that all believers are the salt of the earth:

> You are the light of the world. A town built on a hill cannot be hidden. Neither do
> people light a lamp and put it under a bowl. Instead they put it on its stand, and it
> gives light to everyone in the house. In the same way, let your light shine before
> others, that they may see your good deeds and glorify your Father in heaven
> (Matthew 5:14-16).

In fact, evangelism should be a priority for every organization in the local church.[120] C.E.

Matthews described it this way:

----

[118] Ibid.

[119] Kennedy, *Evangelism Explosion,* 7.

[120] C.E. Matthews, *The Southern Baptist Program of Evangelism* (Atlanta, GA: Home Mission Board, 1949), 3.

> We do not recommend that the soul-winning be done by a hand-picked group of trained workers; we recommend that it by done by every member of the church through our Sunday School, Woman's Missionary Union, Training Union, and Brotherhood. This should include the entire church membership. . . [I]t is the business of the church to do the soul-winning, which does not end with the salvation of a soul but save the life in Christian service in the church.[121]

Kennedy's viewpoint of training a concentrated few differs from Matthews' viewpoint, but we must consider that the logistics of time and physical proximity dictate an extensive training program for a select group. The call for all believers to evangelize remains intact.

Training should operate from a perspective whereby the student imitates the mentor.[122] In John 1:35-51, we find the recorded Scripture where Jesus recruited His disciples. It is interesting to note that these men followed Jesus because they *wanted* to. We could respond on the premise that Christ already put this type of passion in their hearts. Nevertheless, imitation is borne out of a desire to follow someone because the student desires to. Paul had his students in Paphos and Pisidian Antioch (Acts 13:13-14) who followed him. Paul, Silas, and Timothy even referred to those at Thessalonica as being imitators of them (1 Thessalonians 1:6). The personal contact between the student and mentor lends itself to effective training.

Training in the New Testament involved "co-location." It was imperative for Jesus and Paul to stay together with those they mentored.[123] This is in stark contrast to the

---

[121] Ibid.

[122] Finney, *Emerging Evangelism*, 148-149.

[123] Kennedy, *Evangelism Explosion*, 110-115.

types of training available today. But we must consider that the disciples did not have access to laptops or devices. Today, the Internet has only existed for twenty years, so on-line education or even email was not available two thousand years ago. In fact, writing documents involved employing scribes who were highly trained and received the same status as physicians and lawyers.[124] Thus, the preferred method of training was face-to-face.

The biblical mandate for training also required accountability.[125] The aspect of training involved not only intellectual learning, but a lifestyle change. This change was not just intended for one's own personal satisfaction, but to "please God" (1 Thessalonians 4:1). Paul, Silas, and Timothy provided a clear level of accountability in the presence of an omniscient God:

> As for other matters, brothers and sisters, we instructed you how to live in order to please God, as in fact you are living. Now we ask you and urge you in the Lord Jesus to do this more and more. For you know what instructions we gave you by the authority of the Lord Jesus. It is God's will that you should be sanctified; that you should avoid sexual immorality; that each of you should learn to control your own body in a way that is holy and honorable, not in passionate lust like the pagans, who do not know God; and that in this matter no one should wrong or take advantage of a brother or sister. The Lord will punish all those who commit such sins, as we told you and warned you before. For God did not call us to be impure, but to live a holy life. Therefore, anyone who rejects this instruction does not reject a human being but God, the very God who gives you his Holy Spirit (1 Thessalonians 4:1-8).

Therefore, it is appropriate to expect something from those in training.

---

[124] James M. Freeman, *Manners and Customs of the Bible* (Plainfield, NJ: Logos International, 1972), 341-342.

[125] Coleman, *The Master Plan of Evangelism,* 110-115.

Training basically requires endurance.[126] If today's college student desires a degree, then they must endure the required curriculum. Paul's encouragement to Timothy spoke well of this endurance. Paul spoke of his suffering to the extent of being chained, but yet endured for the sake of those coming to Christ:

> Remember Jesus Christ, raised from the dead, descended from David. This is my gospel, for which I am suffering even to the point of being chained like a criminal. But God's word is not chained. Therefore I endure everything for the sake of the elect, that they too may obtain the salvation that is in Christ Jesus, with eternal glory (2 Timothy 2:8-10).

But enduring the mission of proclaiming the gospel was not meant to be a lonely task. Certainly, Jesus ascribed to this when He appointed the twelve apostles to do His work after He ascended into heaven. The apostle Paul also showed concern when he advised Timothy: "Only Luke is with me. Get Mark and bring him with you, because he is helpful to me in my ministry" (2 Timothy 4:11). He also advised Titus in this way: "As soon as I send Artemas or Tychicus to you, do your best to come to me at Nicopolis, because I have decided to winter there. Do everything you can to help Zenas the lawyer and Apollos on their way and see that they have everything they need" (Titus 3:12-13).

Training requires delegation.[127] Is it appropriate for a protégé in ministry to learn the traits of the ministry but not put them into practice? There must be opportunities for the protégé to carry on with the ministry. Paul encouraged Timothy to do this very thing with his protégés: "And the things you have heard me say in the presence of many

---

[126] Ibid.

[127] Ibid.

witnesses entrust to reliable people who will also be qualified to teach others" (2 Timothy

2:2). Conversely, this aspect of delegation is not naturally relished by mentors:

> He [the mentor] is glad to give the responsibility to others but reluctant to let the reins of power slip from his own hands. Also, some leaders feel threatened by brilliant subordinates and therefore are reluctant to delegate authority. Whatever the basic cause, failure to delegate authority is unfair to the subordinate and unlikely to prove satisfactory or effective. Such an attitude tends to be interpreted as indicating a lack of confidence, and that does not promote the best cooperation, nor will it draw out the full abilities of the one being trained for leadership.[128]

Eventually, a lack of delegation will affect the congregation. The gifting and grace

supplied by Christ through the mentor to the protégé is quenched. This approach is not

consistent with Ephesians 4:11 as discussed earlier. God's approach for gifting as noted

in verse 11 is to build up the body of Christ. This requires humility on the part of the

mentor. This is what Paul was referring to in 2 Timothy 2:2 when he said "entrust to

reliable people."

The fruits of training come at a cost. The price of victory is high.[129] As part of

Paul's instruction to Timothy, he encourages him to "join with me in suffering, like a

good soldier of Christ Jesus" (2 Timothy 2:3). The cost of training and executing

evangelism is not just due to the work itself. The gospel is well received by those who are

destined to receive it, but it is received harshly be the world. In an earlier verse (2

Timothy 1:11-12a), Paul wrote Timothy, "And of this gospel I was appointed a herald

and an apostle and a teacher. That is why I am suffering as I am." Jesus, too, reminded

---

[128] J. Oswald Sanders, *Spiritual Leadership: Principles of Excellence for Every Believer* (Chicago, IL: Moody Press, 1994), 137-138.

[129] Coleman, *The Master Plan of Evangelism,* 110-115.

his disciples: "If the world hates you, keep in mind that it hated me first. If you belonged

to the world, it would love you as its own. As it is, you do not belong to the world, but I

have chosen you out of the world. That is why the world hates you" (John 15:18-19).

There is a benefit, however, for those who remain faithful to Christ:

> Do not let your hearts be troubled. You believe in God; believe also in me
> [Christ]. My Father's house has many rooms; if that were not so, would I have
> told you that I am going there to prepare a place for you? And if I go and prepare
> a place for you, I will come back and take you to be with me that you also may be
> where I am (John 14:1-3).

The Cultural Setting for Evangelism

This section focuses on what Christian theologians view as the cultural setting for

evangelism. The categories of evangelism discussed are: (1) the setting, (2) a believer's

response, (3) a church's response, and (4) evangelism vs. the social gospel. The previous

section discussed tangible concepts from Scripture used from a human viewpoint

regarding the mandate for evangelism. This section will develop further Scriptural

analyses from a human viewpoint as we begin to explore how evangelism works on a

daily basis in the western culture.

The setting for evangelism.

The generation of recipients must be taken into account. There are obviously

various generations of recipients in our society, but there is a specific focus on the next

generation. Who will be the Christian witnesses for the next generation? Christianity has endured and grown over the last two millennia, but are we to expect that growth to

continue in the future? George Barna expressed this concern regarding the Bridgers:[130]

> The Bridgers are the first generation of Americans to be raised without the
> cultural presupposition that they would become Christians or explore Christianity.
> Many of the Bridgers take a smorgasbord approach to religion. They take the
> elements of each religion that make them most comfortable. They may even call
> themselves "Christians," but the term is used generically.

This is a very tenuous situation for this generation. No longer is Christianity

systematically imposed or even taught to this generation. Nevertheless, this is the setting

that evangelists are exposed to today.

To understand Bridgers' attitudes about truth, consider Table 4. Clearly, there is a

lack of understanding about truth. Are evangelists aware of this particular generational

Table 4. Bridgers' attitudes about truth[131]

Attitude	Agree	Disagree	Don't Know
What is right for one person is right for another	91%	8%	1%
No one can be absolutely positive they know the truth	80%	19%	1%
There is no "absolute truth"	72%	28%	0%

attitude? How can evangelists minister to theses recipients if they have little regard for an

"absolute truth" such as God's Word? Yet this is the setting for modern day evangelism,

---

[130] George Barna, *Generation Next* (Ventura, CA: Regal, 1995), 74-75.

[131] Ibid., 39.

New Testament Evangelism

and believers need to realize this in order to effectively minister to these recipients. Bill

Moyers looked at it this way: "How can I hold *my* truth [God's Word] to be *the* truth

when so many others see truth so differently?"[132]

Yet, the setting for these recipients becomes even more challenging. What are the

major concerns of these recipients? Do we understand their point of view? Must we

understand their point of view in order to relate to them, particularly, with regard to the

gospel? The major concerns of the Bridgers is shown in Table 5. We notice that the two

major concerns are educational-related and relationships. Perhaps this might segue into

some conversations. Surveying a recipients thoughts in these areas might show love and

concern. This could lead to one person identifying with another. It may lead to a

conversation about the gospel.

Table 5. Bridgers' major concerns[133]

Concern	Percent of Respondents
Educational-related	45%
Relationships	24%
Emotional pressure	17%
Physical threats, violence	13%
Financial difficulties	13%
Substance abuse	11%

[132] Bill Moyers, "America's Religious Mosaic," *USA Weekend* (11-13 October 1996), 5.

[133] Ibid., 120.

Walt Mueller reported similar concerns in Table 6. Mueller's finding report an emphasis on relationships, compared to Barna's. That is not to say that education-related concerns previously reported by Barna are unimportant, however, the peer concerns regarding relationships highlight a biblical principle. People have an underlying need for more intimate (friend) relationships. Interesting enough, God has the same desire when it comes to relationships with believers. That is why He sent His Son Jesus Christ to die on the cross as a sacrificial substitute for our sins, so that we will not encounter eternal death, but rather, an eternal relationship with Jesus Christ Himself. Christ is all about relationships. Perhaps this is a good segue into a conversation with a Bridger about peer concerns.

Table 6. Peer concerns of Bridgers[134]

Concern	Percent of Respondents
My close friends understand me better than my parents	70%
I learn more from my close friends than I do from my parents	70%
I'm more "myself" with my close friends than I am with my parents	68%

More general concerns about Bridgers are:[135]

1. Will something bad happen to my family?

---

[134] Walt Mueller, *Understanding Today's Youth Culture* (Wheaton, IL: Tyndale, 1994), 41.

[135] Thom S. Rainer, *The Bridger Generation* (Nashville, TN: Broadman & Holman Publishers, 1997), 118-130.

2. Will I be able to make it financially?

3. Will I get a good education?

4. Will I be a victim of violence or crime?

5. Will my friends still like me if I don't get along?

6. How do I tell right from wrong?

7. Where will I find time to do everything?

8. Do I have to have sex this young?

9. Will someone I know die from AIDS?

10. Will I have a happy marriage and family?

This list goes beyond relationships and education-related concerns, but it does provide a believer with a perspective from which to identify with the recipient. We note from John 4 that Jesus was quick to identify with the Samaritan woman. He knew she had a concern about relationships as well as her spiritual beliefs. His preparation and readiness to respond to her concerns led to her conversion experience where she placed her trust in Him. Similarly, believers can prepare for their conversations with recipients by understanding their concerns and how they might respond to those concerns.

A believer's response to evangelism.

New Testament Evangelism

In light of the cultural setting, how is a believer to respond to the call to evangelize? The tongue is a powerful tool, but how can it be used to *effectively* share the gospel of Christ? Is a believer at liberty to proclaim Christ to any recipient within hearing distance no matter what they are experiencing? We will explore some areas that a believer can focus on when preparing to share the gospel of Christ.

Consider the example of Philip in Acts 8. Philip headed south from Jerusalem to Gaza on a desert road when he met an Ethiopian eunuch (verses 26-40). The eunuch was reading Scripture and asked Philip a question. Philip shared the gospel of Christ with the eunuch, who then accepted Christ and was baptized. Even though Philip was also ascribed the title, "evangelist," by Luke (Acts 21:8), we note in Acts 8:6-7 that he also performed miracles, healings, and exorcisms. An evangelist is not just an exclusive office, but rather, evangelism is one of several gifts that any one believer may possess in different proportions.

Evangelism is a gift that exists among the laity.[136] Evangelists do not have to be recruited from the clergy. In fact, a number of people are gifted with evangelism. This author noted recently that a couple in the church started a ministry in which they provided warm clothing to a shelter. During the morning when the clothes were distributed, the couple gave Bible tracts to those attending. There were numerous discussions about faith in Christ throughout the morning. Evangelism is a shared practice among all believers.

---

[136] Abraham, *The Logic of Evangelism*, 49.

This may be a daunting statement to some, but according to Donald McGavran, a sign of spiritual renewal in any believer's heart is a passion for the lost.[137] He continued by indicating that one's own spiritual renewal is proportional to one's response to the call for evangelism. The foundation for a relationship in Christ is a person's willingness to share the gospel:[138]

> No one can be *fully* biblically sound and spiritually renewed without being tremendously concerned about the multitudes of unreached men and women and, indeed, of unreached segments of society. It is impossible for anybody to be really in Christ, really full of the *Holy Spirit* [italics mine], without doing what the 120 did on the day of Pentecost. They rushed out and told everyone they met about Jesus and urged them to become his followers.

Would local congregations agree with McGavran? Have those who have ushered the isles of church pews for decades singing God's hymns acknowledge this? The Scripture in Acts 2:1-41 certainly appears to support McGavran's claim. The 120 were "filled with the Holy Spirit" (verse 4). The *Holy Spirit* used this opportunity to speak through Peter as he shared the gospel of Christ to those listening (verses 14-36). This proclamation of Christ led to the conversion (by the *Holy Spirit*) of over three thousand believers. We need to be honest with ourselves. Is our ministry a result of *our* participation with Christ, or is it a result of what the *Holy Spirit* is doing through us?

Granted, the Holy Spirit does endue us with certain gifts with regard to evangelism. Mortimer Aria and Alan Johnson pointed to a compassion for the lost as a

---

[137] McGavran, *Effective Evangelism*, 37.
[138] Ibid.

requirement for evangelism.[139] They maintain that evangelism should not be considered until a believer is truly concerned about others. They reference Matthew 9:36, where Jesus had compassion on the harassed and helpless people who were ostracized from society on a hillside. Jesus was not interested in statistics, but rather peoples' suffering "and their lot in an unjust and oppressive world under false and unreliable leadership."[140] Does this example point to some people we know in our western culture today? Leander Keck observed that "Christians should be characterized by a deep love and compassion for persons whose lives are in disarray because they do not or cannot yet rely on their Creator, are not yet rightly related to their God."[141] People whom Christ would want us to share the gospel with do not carry signs that they want to be evangelized. Rather, their lot in life and their viewpoint of how they are being treated in the world is sufficient signage for us. Therefore, a believer must have a heart for the oppressed.

How a believer conducts their life is a reflection of their faith in Christ. This type of lifestyle is what a recipient sees. Therefore, the goal of each believer is to have a lifestyle that reflects integrity. John Finney summed it up this way, "When Christians show a basic trustworthiness and honesty in their dealings with people they are making a good witness."[142] Integrity prepares a believer for evangelism.

---

[139] Mortimer Aria and Alan Johnson, *The Great Commission: Biblical Models for Evangelism* (Nashville, TN: Abingdon Press, 1992), 28.

[140] Ibid.

[141] Leander E. Keck, *The Church Confident* (Nashville, TN: Abingdon Press, 1993), 116.

[142] Finney, *Emerging Evangelism*, 148-149.

New Testament Evangelism

A believer must also trust God for what He is doing. This is not a trust from a believer's perspective, but rather from God's perspective. Poh Fang Cha put it this way:[143]

> In moments when we don't understand God's ways, we need to trust his unchanging character. That's exactly what Habakkuk did [Habakkuk 1:1-11] . . . In the process, he learned to look at his circumstances from the framework of God's character instead of looking at God's character from the context of his own circumstances.

This necessitates that the believer will focus on their love for Christ, rather than their own methodologies.[144] Are we focused on Christ, or on our own abilities? The apostle John said that "He must increase, and I must decrease" (John 3:30). A believer must look at evangelism from God's point of view and practice accordingly.

A believer should spend time studying the New Testament to determine the right doctrine for evangelism. For example, Jesus' teachings in Matthew 5-7 prepare a believer for not only living a Christian life, but also how to approach sharing the gospel. Jesus declared that the path to eternal life is not obvious to many – "small is the gate and narrow the road that leads to life, and only a few find it" (Matthew 7:14). Jesus then proceeded with the next verse: "Watch out for false prophets." These examples are what Aria and Johnson call orthodoxy or right doctrine.[145] But these principles must result in what they call orthopraxy or right living. It is not enough to understand what needs to be done, but a believer must then act on what they understand. Scriptures related to

---

[143] Poh Fang Chia, "Doesn't God Care?" *Our Daily Bread* 60, no. 6, 17.

[144] J.V. Taylor, *Change of Address* (London: Hodder & Stoughton, 1968), 94-95.

[145] Aria and Johnson, *The Great Commission*, 20-21.

orthopraxy can be found in Matthew 8-9. Jesus told the disciples, "The harvest is

plentiful but the workers are few. Ask the Lord of the harvest, therefore, to send out

workers into his harvest field" (Matthew 9:37-38). In this Scripture, He was referring to

the ostracized previously noted on the hillside. The believer should not only be engaged

in sharing the gospel, but also extensively praying for more resources to do the work.

This was further emphasized when James wrote to the Jewish believers:

> Faith in itself, if it is not accompanied by action, is dead . . . Show me your faith
> without deeds, and I will show you my faith by my deeds . . . Was not our father
> Abraham considered righteous for what he did when he offered his son Isaac on
> the altar? You see that his faith and his actions were working together, and his
> faith was made complete by what he did . . . As the body without the spirit is
> dead, so faith without deeds is dead (James 2:17-26).

Both orthodoxy and orthopraxy reflect not just God's plan for each believer, but what

God requires.

Orthopraxis involves sharing Christ at a personal level. This goes beyond

proclamation (*kerygma*) or teaching (*didache*). Personal evangelism (*martyria*), involves

the "imparting to others of the Christian message in which one's own insights and

convictions play the major role."[146] This is borne out in the gospel being conveyed

through conversation at a deep, personal level. We recall from John 4, that Jesus

conversed with the Samaritan woman at this level. Jesus already knew that the woman

was previously married, and this immediately setup the conversation at a personal level.

At this level, Jesus had the freedom to discuss spiritual things such as living water (verse

----

[146] David Lowes Watson, "Evangelism: A Disciplinary Approach," *International Bulletin of Missionary Research* 7, no. 1 (January 1983), 6.

10). This was of interest to the woman and led to her putting her faith and trust in Him

(verse 15).

Bailey Smith encouraged believers to make evangelism central to their

ministry.[147] If evangelism is viewed as something that a believer "does," then it becomes

peripheral to what they are doing. It needs to be part of a believer's life. The following

are some excuses for not doing evangelism, but they also serve as a check as to whether

or not evangelism is incorporated into one's ministry:

1. Perform discipleship instead

2. Pursue "deeper life"

3. Too busy

4. Cultivating lost friends, but not sharing the gospel

Sharing the gospel should be part of a believer's ministry, without excuse. Jesus said, "If

anyone is ashamed of me and my words in this adulterous and sinful generation, the Son

of Man will be ashamed of them when he comes in his Father's glory with the holy

angels" (Mark 8:38).

Believers must not only have compassion for others in order to evangelize, but

they must work according to the viewpoint of those they are trying to reach. For example,

---

[147] Douglas M. Cecil, review of Bailey E. Smith, *Real Evangelism* (Nashville, TN: Word Publishing, 1999), *Bibliotheca Sacra* 157, no. 628 (October – December 2000), 505.

we note in Acts 17:22-31, that Paul commended the pagans for their desire to worship.[148]

The Athenians were known for their polytheism. Paul realized that if we wanted to share

the gospel, he must first start with the other person's point of view. So he then diverted

their attention to an object of their worship with an inscription to the "UNKNOWN" God

(verse 23). He used this reference as his starting point to share about Christ. He talked

with them based on what he had in common them:[149]

1. They were both religious

2. They both had a desire to worship

3. They both recognized that God is greater than humans

4. They both knew that God is not dependent on gifts from humans

5. They both understood that God does not dwell in temples

6. They both realized the dignity of being human

If we are to effectively reach others with the gospel, we must minister to them in their

setting and their point of view.

Darrell Bock and Mike Del Rosario have a contrasting approach regarding a

believer's response to evangelism. They base their approach on Paul's declaration to the

Corinthians: "By the humility and gentleness of Christ, I appeal to you – I, Paul, who am

---

[148] Barrs, *The Heart of Evangelism,* 204-206.
[149] Ibid.

New Testament Evangelism

'timid' when face to face with you, but 'bold' toward you when away" (2 Corinthians 10:1). They summarized this verse into the following actions for sharing the gospel:[150]

1. We are ambassadors

2. We are to be humble

3. We must use an appropriate tone

The concept of an ambassador might seem ambiguous, but Bock and Del Rosario further define an ambassador as one who must "interact with the culture, engage with the culture, understand its hopes, its aspirations . . . its language, and then being able to communicate the gospel in a way that connects right where they live."[151]

The point on humility must also be further defined. The believer must leave the recipient with a proper perspective about himself.[152] The recipient does not want to be another person talked to, but someone who is valued. They should feel this way about the believer: "He may be challenging me, but there's no doubt he cares about me while he's issuing the challenge."[153]

This type of care must be conveyed in the tone that is used. This is the actual medium used in the conversation, and eventually, the conveyance of the gospel. Bock and Del Rosario stated that "I [the believer] must communicate some level of respect so they

---

[150] Darrell L. Bock and Mike Del Rosario, "The Table Briefing: Tone and Truth in Cultural Engagement," *Bibliotheca Sacra* 173 (January – March, 2016), 99-104.

[151] Ibid., 100.

[152] Ibid., 102.

[153] Ibid.

know I care and then they will listen."[154] If we are to effectively minister to others with the gospel, we must minister to them in *their* setting.

In addition to the tone, the believer must engage the recipient in the conversation. One way to engage them is to ask questions. Asking questions gives the believer an opportunity to learn the recipient's heart and mind and to show love and concern.[155] The focus of the evangelism is not on the believer, but on the recipient. Once love and concern are shown to the recipient, they will be more apt to engage in conversation. In a one-hour meeting with a client, Francis Schaffer would spend 55 minutes asking questions and 5 minutes trying to say something.[156] Asking questions has a way of ministering to others in *their* setting.

Another method of engaging the recipient in conversation is to build bridges.[157] Again, this put an emphasis on the recipient; *their* values and concerns are important. The apostle Paul used this technique when he engaged the residents at Pisidian Antioch. He commended those in the synagogue for their recognition of God's work with the nation of Israel spanning the time from the Exodus to the time of David. After getting their attention, he concluded his discourse with these words: "Therefore, my friends, I want you to know that through Jesus the forgiveness of sins is proclaimed to you. Through him everyone who believes is set free from every sin, a justification you were not able to

---

[154] Ibid., 104.

[155] Jerram Barrs, *The Heart of Evangelism* (Wheaton, IL: Crossway Books, 2011), 225.

[156] Ibid.

[157] Ibid., 203-204.

obtain under the law of Moses" (Acts 13:38-39). The response of those in the synagogue

was to invite Paul and Barnabas back to the synagogue the following Sabbath!

But Paul went deeper in his discourse to those at Antioch. He focused on what he

and the recipients had in common. Jerram Barrs dissociated the discourse in Acts 13:38-

39 into the following commonalities:[158]

1. They believed in the one, true God

2. They were familiar with the Old Testament

3. They knew the history of Israel

4. They were committed to obeying the Torah

5. They expected the Messiah

6. They respected the forthcoming Judgment day

7. They knew John the Baptist

8. They knew about Jesus

These commonalities are another way to help a believer to effectively minister to a

recipient in *their* setting.

A believer must keep a proper focus when it comes to evangelism. The number of

conversions is not a concern for the believer.[159] The only concern for the believer is to

---

[158] Ibid.

share the gospel, and if necessary, build relationships which will later lead to an opportunity to share the gospel. According to the apostle Paul, it is the Holy Spirit that performs the work of conversion in an unbeliever's heart: "I want you to know that no one who is speaking by the Spirit of God says, 'Jesus is Lord,' except by the Holy Spirit" (1 Corinthians 12:3).

A local church's response to evangelism.

In light of the cultural setting, how is a local church to respond to the call to evangelize? Should the local church take direct responsibility for evangelism, or does this responsibility fall on others? Would it be appropriate to have just a few members in the local church practice evangelism, or should it be the character of the local church?

Carl Braaten puts the emphasis of God's Kingdom work on the local church in the present, rather than in the future.[160] Christ's forgiveness of sins and restoration of a broken relationship with God are happening now. The church is the medium through which God is performing His missional work.[161] We cannot escape the conclusion that God uses the Church to bring sinners to Himself. This missional work is distributed from the Church as Christ's body to the individual local churches. It is an active work which requires immediacy on the part of the local church.

---

[159] Abraham, *The Logic of Evangelism,* 47.

[160] Carl E. Braaten, *"The Meaning of Evangelism in the Context of God's Universal Grace,"* in *The Story of Evangelism: Exploring a Missional Practice of the Church,* ed. Paul W. Chilcote and Laceye C. Warner (Grand Rapids, MI: William B. Eerdmans Publishing Company, 2008), 163.

[161] Ibid.

Is this immediacy counter-cultural in the Church today? God's Word is clear that there should be an immediacy to share the gospel, since unrepentant sin leads to eternal destruction (Romans 6:23a). The solution for this is eternal life through Jesus Christ (Romans 6:23b). Mark McCloskey claimed that first century converts came to a faith in Christ because they could see drastic changes in their lives – either physical or spiritual healings, which moved them to a faith that saved their souls from eternal destruction.[162] McCloskey continued:

> This perspective is lacking in today's evangelical circles . . . The result is sort of a spiritual truce: They don't bother us, and we won't bother them . . . we have unconsciously succumbed to the spirit of 'non-cruciality' fueled by those assumptions having permeated our culture.[163]

Does this match up with Romans 6:23 regarding the wages of sin is death? Is an attitude of apathy towards unbelievers an appropriate interpretation of this portion of Scripture? To counter this level of apparent apathy, McCloskey turned to 2 Corinthians 5:11-21 to realize "that God was reconciling the world to himself in Christ" (verse 19).

Historically, the Church of Christ has grown over the centuries due to evangelism. This drew Donald McGavran to make the following conclusion:[164]

> Every great expansion of the church in all ages has depended upon the Word being spread by believing Christians of all ranks. Conversely, whenever evangelism has been held to be the work solely of trained evangelists and paid pastors, their denominations have grown slowly or have become static or declined.

---

[162] Mark McCloskey, *Tell it Often – Tell it Well* (San Bernardino, CA: Here's Life Publishers, 1985), 132.

[163] Ibid., 132-135.

[164] McGavran, *Effective Evangelism*, 50.

Church growth, therefore, requires an active response on the part of local churches to continue this Kingdom growth.

This missional work for the local church is to "create a community of Kingdom people."[165] If we reference Matthew 28 which specifies the making of disciples, we must assert that this process of making disciples begins with a conversion of the heart. The conversion of the heart, however, is based on the sharing of the gospel, or evangelism. The Kingdom perspective, therefore, is for the local church to be effective in evangelism in order to provide the gospel message.

Church growth is simply a result of faithfulness to the Great Commission in Matthew 28.[166] This is how the Church has existed and grown over the last two millennium. It is a result of the grace of God, as empowered by the Holy Spirit, upon believers who remain faithful to that Great Commission. This process is a result of sanctification in believers, so "as a church grows in faith and knowledge, it increases its ability to impact the world for Christ."[167] The antithesis is also true: if a church is not impacting the world for Christ, it is limited in faith and knowledge. Believers have true spiritual growth when they participate in evangelism.

---

[165] Johnson, *Rethinking Evangelism*, 121.

[166] James Emery White, *Opening the Front Door: Worship and Church Growth* (Nashville, TN: Convention Press, 1992), 14.

[167] Ibid.

New Testament Evangelism

Braaten argued that local church evangelism is both a privilege and an obligation

for the early local churches:[168]

> Christians who existed among Jews and Gentiles understood that it was the gospel
> that made the difference and that belief in this gospel meant the privilege and
> obligation to make it known to all others. The successors of the apostles had to
> continue doing what the apostles had begun.

The apostle Paul emphasized this with the Romans:

> How, then, can they call on the one they have not believed in? And how can they
> believe in the one of whom they have not heard? And how can they hear without
> someone preaching to them? And how can anyone preach unless they are sent? As
> it is written: 'How beautiful are the feet of those who bring good news!' (Romans
> 10:14-15).

This Scripture clearly puts the emphasis of evangelism on the local church. If the local

church does not claim this responsibility, then who else will? God has chosen the local

church to participate with Him in this responsibility; it is a privilege as well as an

obligation.

Each church must discern the needs of the community before ministering to it.

The local church or churches would then be considered relevant.[169] This is an artifact of

interpersonal communication. If one person wants to not only engage another person in

dialogue but wants to serve that person in some way, they must generate some interest in

a topic that is important to the other person. This is why just sharing the gospel during a

door-to-door visitation may not interest the recipient. The believer sharing the gospel

---

[168] Carl E. Braaten, *"The Meaning of Evangelism in the Context of God's Universal Grace,"* in *The Story of Evangelism: Exploring a Missional Practice of the Church,* ed. Paul W. Chilcote and Laceye C. Warner (Grand Rapids, MI: William B. Eerdmans Publishing Company, 2008), 162.

[169] Green, *Evangelism through the Local Church,* 101.

must first generate some interest or some reason why the recipient might listen to the

gospel – and some reason that is important to them. One way of doing this is for the

believer to ask the recipient if there is need that they can pray about. This would allow

the recipient to bring forward something that is important to them. It can also lead to a

conversation about the gospel after the need is prayed for.

We must take note that there are sometimes obstacles to the mission of

evangelism in the local church. Pride is the antithesis of love (1 Corinthians 13:4), yet it

can lead to conflict (Proverbs 13:10). In this case, pride can prevent a local church from

exercising local evangelism. David Roper noted that "quarrels are fueled by pride, by

needing to be right, by wanting our way, or by defending our turf or our egos."[170] Where

this occurs in the local church, there will surely be an impact on evangelism. The local

church has a responsibility to incorporate evangelism along with the other gifts, but it

must be careful to root out pride in the local church body.

Ben Johnson also concurred that perceived power among the believers in a church

is proportional to the hindrance of evangelism.[171] As mentioned previously, pride is the

antithesis of love, which limits the unity of the church. If the local church is indeed going

to come together to perform evangelism, it must root out any pride that exists. The

emphasis here should be on the unity of the local church which makes it effective in the

community.

------

[170] David Roper, "The Two Bears," *Our Daily Bread* 60, no. 8 (August 2015), 12.

[171] Johnson, *Rethinking Evangelism*, 84-85.

Joseph Tyson also subscribed to unity as being an effective tool for ministry. He issued the following statement:[172]

> The problem that Paul faced in writing 1 Corinthians was that of creating unity in a situation where none had previously existed . . . His main concern and stress in the letter are on the unity of the church and the legitimate role that *all* [italics mine] members play. On the question of spiritual gifts, he says, 'Now there are varieties of gifts, but the same Spirit; and there are varieties of service, but the same Lord' (1 Corinthians 12:4-5). He stresses the unity of the church in saying, 'Now you are the body of Christ and individually members of it' (1 Corinthians 12:27).

The local church, therefore, has a responsibility to incorporate evangelism with other gifts, but only in the context of unity with all members of the local church.

One method of incorporating evangelism is to have an evangelistic group within the local church focused on outreach.[173] This group would not only operate in obedience to God's Word, but would operate in a pragmatic fashion: "Let the ardent Christians form missionary groups of evangelistic bands that will meet once a week or once a month to make sure that 'our congregation does win the lost in our community and give birth to daughter congregations at home and abroad.'"[174] Thus, the incorporation of evangelism leads to Church growth. This is not just necessarily a constant monitoring of numbers of believers in each congregation, but a realization that the overall Church is growing according to Christ's plan.

---

[172] Joseph B. Tyson, *The New Testament and Early Christianity* (New York, NY: MacMillan Publishing Company, 1984), 325.

[173] McGavran, *Effective Evangelism*, 46.

[174] Ibid.

From a broader perspective, the local church has specific resources that it offers. George Hunter assimilated these as shown in Table 7. The church's resources). The initial resource of the local church is the proclamation of the gospel. A recipient's response to this is repentance and a subsequent relationship with Christ. The next resource is fellowship. This results in a unified body of believers. The final resource for a local church is service. The result of this is that the world is impacted for Christ. Interesting enough, we see a cyclical pattern here. When the world is impacted for Christ, other recipients are then available to hear the gospel. The local church's resources and the subsequent responses of the recipients keeps repeating itself over and over again. This expanded definition of resources and responses defines evangelism from an operational point of view. It describes how the local church operates with respect to evangelism as a perpetual activity.

Table 7. The church's resources[175]

Church's Resource	Recipient's Response
Kerygma (message)	To Christ
Koinonia (fellowship)	To the Christian congregation
Diakonia (service)	To the world

This perpetual activity calls for pastors and church leaders to lead the effort of evangelism.[176] This requires leaders to participate in evangelism so that this role model

---

[175] Hunter, *The Contagious Congregation*, 31.

will be perpetuated to the members of the congregation. How can the members put a

precedence on evangelism if the leaders are not actively witnessing? This extends to the

pulpit. Malcolm McDow and Alvin Reid came to this conclusion:[177]

> The effective leader hears God's voice when all other ears are deaf. He hears
> God's call, is unwavering in his commitment, and unexplainable in human
> rationale in his power with people. God has touched him, and God uses him to
> touch others. The burden of revival is upon him; there is 'fire in his bones,' and he
> can do no other than to preach the message of renewal that God has laid upon his
> soul. Pastors must engage in evangelism out of obedience to Christ or their
> spiritual lives risk becoming powerless.[178]

In addition, all members in a local church must participate in evangelism.[179] This

falls under Jesus' command to Simon, "From now on you will fish for people" (Luke

5:10). The effort of performing evangelism is not a human one, but a divine one. Jesus

told the disciples that "whoever believes in me will do the works I have been doing, and

they will do even greater things than these, because I am going to the Father . . . If you

love me, keep my commands" (John 14:12-15). The enabling of believers to perform this

work was given by Christ "to equip his people for works of service, so that the body of

Christ may be built up" (Ephesians 4:11). Therefore, "all [believers] are ministering

---

[176] Timothy Beougher and Alvin Reid, eds., *Evangelism for a Changing World* (Wheaton, IL: Harold Shaw Publishers, 1995), 114.

[177] Malcolm McDow and Alvin Reid, *Firefall: How God has Shaped History through Revivals* (Nashville, TN: Broadman & Holman Publishers, 1997), 11.

[178] Beougher and Reid, *Evangelism for a Changing World*, 114.

[179] Coleman, *Evangelism in Perspective,* 45.

servants and have the same mandate to make disciples."[180] Paul Chilcote and Laceye

Warner put more of an emphasis on the individual believers within the local church:[181]

> Evangelism is a missional practice of the whole people of God. Evangelism is not simply an activity; it is a set of practices – a habituated way of being in community. While some persons may be particularly gifted as evangelists within the community of faith, God claims all of God's children as 'evangel bearers' for the purpose of God's mission and shalom in the world.

When the emphasis of evangelism is upon every believer within the church, the function of evangelism within the local church is realized. It becomes part of the culture of the local church.

Each believer within the church is a contributor and builds and works to build up the local body. Paul puts it this way to the Ephesians, "From him [Christ] the whole body, joined and held together by every supporting ligament, grows and builds itself up in love, as each part does its work" (Ephesians 4:16). When the majority of believers are actively participating in evangelism, the local church either remains or becomes healthy.[182] It is understandable that there are some believers who are new to the faith, and therefore, have not yet adopted evangelism as part of their lifestyle. But that is where the majority of believers in that church, who have adopted evangelism, can help support and nurture the new believers.

---

[180] Ibid.

[181] Chilcote, Paul W. and Laceye C. Warner, eds., *The Study of Evangelism: Exploring a Missional Practice of the Church* (Grand Rapids, MI: William B. Eerdmans Publishing Company, 2008), xxvi.

[182] Joseph C. Aldrich, *Lifestyle Evangelism: Crossing Traditional Barriers to Reach the Unbelieving World* (Portland, OR: Multnomah Press, 1978), 103.

A healthy church is one in which evangelism is part of its culture. Dallas Willard noted that "if those in the churches really are enjoying fullness of life, evangelism will be unstoppable and largely automatic. The local assembly, for its part, can then become an academy where people throng from the surrounding community to learn how to *live*."[183] In this environment, believers will feel comfortable inviting and receiving visitors in the church, and visitors will feel comfortable in coming out to church. This describes a vibrant culture for the local church where its members are naturally sharing the gospel.

John Finney called a group of believers in a geographical area seeking to minister to people in that area as the "Incarnation Community."[184] The cyclical activity noted earlier (Table 7) whereby a local church proclaims the gospel, engages in fellowship, and performs service is a function of this type of community. The focus here is not on the local church or its members, but rather the residents and workers in the local community. Finney believed that this was Christ's model for the Church.[185]

Evangelism versus the social gospel.

How do we dissociate between evangelism and the social gospel? Is it possible to intermingle the message of Christ as a result of evangelism with various ministries which are the result of the social gospel?

---

[183] Dallas Willard, *The Spirit of the Disciplines: Understanding How God Changes Lives* (San Francisco, CA: Harper & Row Publishers, 1988), 247.

[184] Finney, *Emerging Evangelism*, 112.

[185] Ibid.

William Abraham provided a couple of definitions in this area. He described

evangelism as the "spreading of the good news by proclamation."[186] This is a very simple

definition, but to the point. It leaves some room as to *how* the good news is spread, but

does not limit the method. This definition also does not indicate any expectations on the

part of the recipient, or whether or not there is a single recipient or a group of recipients.

It merely indicates that the good news is sent forward. Abraham also described mission

as the "outflow of the love of God in and through our life, word and deed."[187] This

definition of mission is the social side of what believers do, or what some call the *social

gospel*. We see a contrast here between evangelism and the social gospel. Evangelism is

concerned with the message, whereas, mission or social gospel is concerned with the love

of Christ that is poured out into the community. Roger Bruns noted that Billy Sunday had

some strong words about the social gospel:[188]

> To Billy, the social gospel was yet another liberal, modernist upsurge against
> orthodox, conservative American values and Christian tradition, It was a drive to
> move Christianity away from its principal mission – to save souls; it was
> dominated by intellectual religious meddlers; it was antithetical to the American
> capitalist system; it promoted philosophies such as socialism; it relegated
> Christianity to a social reform agency; it was a sacrilegious quackery; it was, the
> evangelist said, 'godless social service nonsense.'

It seems that that evangelism and the social gospel, however, naturally occur

together. In contrast, Bock and Del Rosario feel that the Church is in "divorce between

----

[186] Abraham, *The Logic of Evangelism,* 46.

[187] Ibid.

[188] Roger A. Bruns, *Preacher: Billy Sunday & Big-Time American Evangelism* (New York, NY: W.W. Norton & Company, 1992), 130.

word and ministry."[189] They maintain that those believers involved in evangelism have a

singular focus for evangelism. Conversely, those believers that have a focus for the social

gospel are not mindful of evangelism. Bock and Del Rosario's point is that evangelism

and the social gospel should be "wedded together."[190] Jesus indicated that evangelism

and the social gospel go together when He said, "I have testimony weightier than that of

John. For the works that the Father has given me to finish – the very works that I am

doing – testify that the Father has sent me" (John 5:36). He demonstrated this in Luke 4

when He spoke the Word from Isaiah 58 and 61 and then said, "The Lord has anointed

me to release the captives." Then in Capernaum, He met the needs of the people. John

Stott put it this way:[191]

> Although reconciliation with man is not reconciliation with God, nor is social
> action evangelism, nor is political liberation salvation, nevertheless we affirm that
> evangelism and socio-political involvement are both part of our Christian duty.
> For both are necessary expressions of our doctrines of God and man, our love for
> our neighbor and our obedience to Jesus Christ.

Believers must obtain an integrated focus of both evangelism and the social gospel in

order to minister effectively. The two must be integrated together.

When it comes to weaving the social gospel and evangelism together, we must

consider that one's gift(s) play an important role in evangelism. In fact, gifting results in

---

[189] Bock and Del Rosario, "The Table Briefing," 98.

[190] Ibid.

[191] John Stott, *The Lausanne Covenant: An Exposition and Commentary* (Minneapolis, MN: World Wide
Publications, 1975), 20.

effective evangelism.[192] This is consistent with Ephesians 4:11, which describes that

gifting directly results in the building up of the Church. These spiritual gifts are the result

of the grace of God, as opposed to the travail of people. This is why Ephesians 2:8-9

proclaims, "For it is by grace you have been saved, through faith – and this not from

yourselves, it is the gift of God – not by works, so that no one can boast." It is where

human beings participate with God in a spiritual matter – the proclamation of Christ's

gospel. The divine to human interface is the empowering of the Holy Spirit in

conjunction with the spiritual gifts provided to engage in evangelism.

We can also look to evangelical leaders to see how they modeled the weaving of

the social gospel and evangelism together. Some of the great evangelical leaders took

note of the conditions in slum areas and responded to the physical needs of those living in

those areas. Leaders such as F.B. Meyer, John Jowett, Charles Spurgeon, and T. deWitt

Talmage established gospel missions, employment bureaus, orphanages, and other

organizations to meet the needs of these people.[193] In addition, fifty evangelical leaders

from six continents[194] met on June 16-23, 1982 at the Reformed Bible College in Grand

Rapids, Michigan for the Consultation on the Relationship between Evangelism and

Social Responsibility (CRESR), co-sponsored by the Lausanne Committee for World

---

[192] John Wimber and Kevin Springer, *Power Evangelism* (San Francisco, CA: Harper & Row Publishers, 1986), xx.

[193] David O. Moberg, *The Great Reversal: Evangelism and Social Concern*, rev. ed. (Philadelphia, PA: J.B. Lippincott Company, 1977), 28-29.

[194] These delegates were comprised of: theologians, pastors, evangelists, missiologists, and social service and development workers. More than half were from third world countries.

New Testament Evangelism

Evangelism and the World Evangelical Fellowship.[195] After a week of intense group

discussions, they came to the conclusion that evangelism and social concern are linked in

the following ways:[196]

1. Christian social concern is a *consequence* of evangelism

2. Christian social concern can be a *bridge* to evangelism

3. Christian social concern should be a *partner* of evangelism

If evangelism is performed the way Jesus intended, we must come to the conclusion that

it will result in social concern. We can look no further than the model Jesus established in

Matthew 9 when he ministered to those on the hillside who were ostracized from society.

He had a concern for both their physical and their spiritual needs when He said, "The

harvest is plentiful but the workers are few. Ask the Lord of the harvest, therefore, to

send out more workers into His harvest field" (Matthew 9:37-38). We also realize from

John 4 that social concern can be a bridge to evangelism. In this passage, Jesus conversed

with a Samaritan woman about thirst. This led to the sharing of Himself (the gospel) to

her, to which she put her faith and trust in Him. The aspect of social concern partnering

with evangelism was also accomplished by Jesus in the gospels. We note from Mark

10:46-52, that the blind Bartimaeus called upon Jesus: "Jesus, Son of David, have mercy

on me!" Jesus asked what He could do for him, and the man indicated that he wanted to

---

[195] Bruce J. Nichols, ed., *In Word and Deed: Evangelism and Social Responsibility* (Grand Rapids, MI: William B. Eerdmans Publishing Company, 1985), 7-8.
[196] Ibid.

New Testament Evangelism

see. Jesus healed him, and said to him, "Go, your faith has healed you." How about the

paralyzed man who was lowered in a stretcher from a roof because of the crowds. His

determination and faith in Christ resulted in this statement from Jesus: "Friend, your sins

are forgiven" (Luke 5:20). Jesus later instructed the paralyzed man in verse 24 to take his

mat and go home. These examples demonstrate that social concern or social gospel is not

void of evangelism, but works in tandem with it.

The Techniques used for Evangelism

This section focuses on what Christian theologians view as the techniques used

for evangelism. The categories under techniques discussed are: (1) conducting outreach,

(2) the plan for evangelism, and (3) a survey for evangelism. The previous section

discussed Scriptural analyses from a human viewpoint as we began to explore how

evangelism works on a daily basis in the western culture. This section will develop

practical approaches to performing evangelism primarily at the local church level.

Conducting outreach.

Armstrong worked extensively with an outreach program at the Presbyterian

Church of Philadelphia in the 1950's and 1960's. From his experience, each church

should have its own outreach program.[197] Each local church is located in a unique setting

as compared with other churches. Therefore, the cultural dynamics will be different. For

---

[197] Armstrong, *Service Evangelism*, 178.

example, we know that each believer that comes into a local church has different (unique) gifts. No two people are exactly alike, so the dynamics that result from a particular believer in a particular local church are unique. The collection of unique believers in a local church results in a unique local church. Therefore, we would expect that the outreach concerns and potential for that local church to be unique from any other local church.

Bock and Del Rosario presented an approach to assist local churches in developing their own unique outreach program. After encouraging local churches to continually pray regarding outreach, they set forth the following parameters for any outreach program:[198]

1. Be faithful in the proclamation of Christ

2. Be faithful in the display of grace through Christ

3. Serve the community

4. Speak on how God cares for people around them

5. Engage in the ministry of the Word and deed

Proclamation is essential to outreach. At some point, the gospel must be presented. In planning for outreach, this component must be included in the program. The "display of grace" requires the local church to be considerate as to how they present their outreach to

---

[198] Bock and Del Rosario, "The Table Briefing," 98.

the community. We want the recipients in the community to be respected and valued during the outreach process. The local church must, according to Bock and Del Rosario, be involved in serving the community. How will the recipients receive love and care unless they are served? The local church must demonstrate to the recipients that God does care for them. This is a sharp distinction between the social gospel and evangelism. The local church is not merely handing out backpacks, for example, to help families prepare their children for school. Rather, it should be performed in conjunction with a demonstration as to how God cares for the families as well. The local church must also adhere to God's Word as they engage in this ministry. The local church must not only look out after their own interests, but also the interests of others (Philippians 2:4). These pointers from Bock and Del Rosario should be considered by the local church in order to effectively develop an appropriate outreach program.

The aspect of boldness should be applied when developing a program for outreach.[199] Peter and John, after being disciplined by the Sanhedrin, returned to the believers and prayed in the following manner: "Why do the nations rage and the peoples plot in vain? The kings of the earth rise up and the rulers band together against the Lord and against his anointed one" (Acts 4:25-26). They then continued in prayer: "Now, Lord, consider their threats and enable our servants to speak your word with great boldness" (verse 29). After they prayed, the place where they were meeting was shaken "and they were all filled with the Holy Spirt and spoke the word of God boldly" (verse

---

[199] Ibid., 97-98.

31). Isn't that how the local church should respond when developing their outreach program? It should be with all fierceness, because that is the type of God we serve!

This boldness is required when inviting recipients to come out to Sunday services. A church in Indiana invited a stonemason from Chicago to come and preach.[200] Upon arrival, the stonemason took a deacon with him to perform door-to-door visitations. He gave a "tender exhortation,"[201] prayed when appropriate, and invited the family to the church services. Within three to four days, others from the church joined in with the visitation. Eventually, scores of believers were performing visitations and hundreds of new visitors were attending services.

Robert Coleman focused on the concept of person to person invitations rather than preaching to the multitudes.[202] We know from John 4, that Jesus preferred speaking to the Samaritan woman at the well rather than going into the town of Sychar to preach to the multitudes. He used the woman's personal history and set of beliefs as a way to speak to her about Himself. It would not be the same if He attempted to speak to the multitude at Sychar, because each person has a unique personal history and beliefs. From a personal standpoint, it may have been difficult for Him to share about Himself to all of the townspeople at Sychar at the same time. Therefore, each local church should conduct outreach on a personal level as part of their outreach effort.

---

[200] Fish and Conant, *Every Member Evangelism for Today,* 24-25.

[201] Ibid.

[202] Coleman, *The Master's Way of Personal Evangelism,* 14.

Coleman further ascribed that the Holy Spirit governs the effort of planning and conducting evangelism rather than church committees.[203] "Only to the degree that we allow the Spirit to exalt Christ in and through us," wrote Coleman, "can our labors bring forth any fruit."[204] This is an overarching concern in the local church. Are the efforts both inside and outside of the local church planned and conducted by human wisdom or in conjunction with the Spirit? Do both the leaders of these efforts as well as the believers who are involved in them realize this? Is it being taught and preached accordingly? Human wisdom cannot affect what Christ does in His work. The apostle Paul wrote that "No one can say, 'Jesus is Lord,' except by the Holy Spirit" (1 Corinthians 12:3). Thus, each local church is unique in its plan to conduct outreach, but that effort must be sensitive to the Holy Spirit.

The planning of outreach needs to take into consideration that the believers in the local church must go out and meet the non-believers in their setting. Ronald Runyon called this effort "community-centered" rather than "church-centered."[205] His premise was that recipients are more comfortable in their setting rather than a church setting. It is one thing for them to have to cross the spiritual threshold of a new life in Christ, but it is quite another when they have to cross the physical threshold of entering a building where they do not know anyone. This gives the recipient an opportunity to focus on Christ,

---

[203] Ibid., 11-12.

[204] Ibid.

[205] Ronald D. Runyon, "Principles and Methods of Household Evangelism," *Bibliotheca Sacra* 142, no. 565 (January-March 1985), 70.

rather than being concerned about being recruited into a church.[206] Runyon is more focused on what he called "household evangelism"[207], a term he ascribed to sharing the gospel and helping new converts in their homes rather than in a church building. There is no Greek word for household. When Cornelius described those people in his house that were devout (*oikos*) in Acts 10:2, he was referring to those in his family or clan.[208] This is in reference to family, friends, and associates or "one's sphere of influence."[209] John Finney described a similar concept called a nurture group.[210] A nurture group is a small group of people who meet at a specific location for a specific purpose. The key components of a nurture group are the following:[211]

1. It is built upon relationships

2. The setting is relaxed, but with a goal

3. It is group-based but not church-linked

4. It does not dictate how people find God (i.e., it allows for unique conversion experiences)

---

[206] Ibid.

[207] Ibid.

[208] Calvin Brown, ed., *New International Dictionary of New Testament Theology* (Grand Rapids, MI: Zondervan Publishing House, 1976), 247-250.

[209] Ibid.

[210] Finney, *Emerging Evangelism*, 82-85.

[211] Ibid.

5. It blends reason with experience (i.e. it blends gospel teaching with the

    articulation of personal experiences)

This is in contrast to the account that was referenced earlier by Fish and Conant, who

subscribed to door-to-door visitations with the intention of inviting the recipients to the

church service. Which method should a local church consider for outreach? Again, that

comes back to the concept that outreach is conducted in concert with the Holy Spirit, and

not just human wisdom from human authors. From this perspective, each local church is

unique with its believers, their spiritual maturity level, and the unique community setting

that they work in. *The Spirit then empowers each local church in their unique setting.*

Whether a local church conducts outreach in homes or from visitations, believers

must keep in mind that relationships are an important component of sharing the gospel. In

a study reported by John Finney, 80% of new believers claimed that relationships were an

important factor in their conversion to Christ.[212] Of these respondents, 25% claimed that

one person was important in their conversion experience; 75% of the respondents claimed

that multiple people helped the recipient in their decision. The key take away is that we

do not know for sure how the Spirit will work in a recipient's heart during the conversion

process to Christ. What is important, however, is that the Spirit works in conjunction with

relationships, or simply, personal contacts.

Outreach should be conducted with the local neighborhood culture in mind. How

else can we reach them unless we take into account their own behaviors and values? Luke

_____

[212] Ibid., 136.

New Testament Evangelism

recounted the story in Acts 17 where Paul addressed the Thessalonians, the Bereans, and

the Athenians. The Thessalonians in the Jewish synagogue were not all open-minded to

the gospel message. By contrast, the Bereans in the Jewish synagogue were open to the

gospel and "received the message with great eagerness and examined the Scriptures every

day" (Acts 17:11). The people of Athens knew nothing about Christ, yet Paul addressed

them according to the altar they had erected "TO AN UNKOWN GOD" (Acts 17:23).

Paul had to react differently in each situation based on the values of the people he was

addressing. D.A. Carson wrote:

> There is a fundamental difference between trying to learn from Acts 17 how to be
> culture-sensitive as we go about declaring the good news of Jesus Christ to people
> who are perishing without him, and thinking of the church as a corporation that
> must market its product to potential consumers. Crossing the cultural barriers to
> communicate the gospel 'that was once for all entrusted to the saints' (Jude 3) is
> one thing. But as we have seen, if we control our evangelism by analysis of
> market 'needs' the result is virtually always a domesticated gospel.[213]

We must address the cultural barriers that exist in our local neighborhoods if we are

going to reach recipients with the gospel. For example, a local church could develop

outreach by taking a survey from the local residents. Some of these questions could be

posed: How good do you think you are on a scale of 1 to 10? What do you think the

consequences are for sin? Have you heard the story of Jesus Christ? Just asking these

three questions to each recipient in the neighborhood will help develop a picture of their

culture and their values. This should help guide the believer, in an Acts 17 fashion, to

address these recipients with the gospel.

---

[213] D.A. Carson, *The Gagging of God: Christianity Confronts Pluralism* (Grand Rapids, MI: Zondervan
Publishing House, 1996), 465-466.

Once the cultural barriers and values of the local neighborhood have been identified, the local church should develop outreach using a model of what George Peters called "saturation evangelism."[214] This is a concept where the church moves outside of the building to share the gospel. This type of outreach is a conglomeration of simultaneous planning activities:[215]

1. Organizational meetings

2. Orientation sessions

3. Inspirational programs

4. Intensive instruction

5. Prayer cells

6. Meetings with a concentrated evangelical thrust

This invokes a more thorough preparation, rather than saying, "Hey, let's do a car wash!" This type of outreach changes the way believers in a local church think about Christianity and how they practice it. It changes the way we "do church." With a comprehensive planning strategy, the focus automatically shifts to the local neighborhood and their need to hear the gospel message.

---

[214] Getz, G.A., review of George W. Peters, *Saturation Evangelism* (Grand Rapids, MI: Zondervan Publishing House, 1970), *Bibliotheca Sacra* 128, no. 510 (April – June 1971), 153-154.
[215] Ibid.

As mentioned earlier, Ronald Runyon advocated what he called "household evangelism."[216] This is a more personal approach for developing outreach compared to George Peter's "saturation evangelism." With household evangelism, a believer develops a strategy based on their sphere of influence. This strategy could be developed in the following fashion:[217]

1. Read an appropriate Scripture

2. Pray

3. List people groups in sphere of one's influence

4. Select an appropriate method for each group

5. Form a team of believers to support one particular group

6. Schedule and implement group meetings for six months

7. Follow-up with new believers and assimilate them into the church

For a local church that is fully committed to evangelism, conducting outreach based on both household evangelism and saturation evangelism is certainly possible. In fact, one of the outcomes of saturation evangelism could be household evangelism.

---

[216] Runyon, "Principles and Methods of Household Evangelism," 73.
[217] Ibid.

When developing outreach, the local church should focus on a long-term approach.[218] It may take several exposures to the gospel for a recipient to come to Christ.[219] We do not know how the Holy Spirit will work in a person's heart. They may hear the gospel and repent of their sins and put their trust in Christ at the first hearing of the gospel. Or, it may take a number of occasions while attending a home study group. Since God works in numerous ways to convict a person's heart, the local church should entertain a number of opportunities to present the gospel.

Therefore, the local church should consider multiple venues when addressing outreach. Michael Green proposed the following three settings for guidance:[220]

1. Public evangelism

2. Personal evangelism

3. Household evangelism

Public evangelism would occur in group settings. These are events where a number of members of the local church come into contact with the community (e.g. Chamber of Commerce events, block parties, and nursing homes). Personal evangelism would be accomplished in a one-on-one setting. This could be just sharing the gospel with a friend or an associate. Household evangelism, as previously mentioned, occurs within one's

---

[218] Jim Peterson, *Evangelism as a Lifestyle* (Colorado Springs, CO: NavPress, 1980), 64-82.
[219] Ibid.
[220] Michael Green, *Evangelism in the Early Church* (Grand Rapids, MI: Eerdmans, 1970), 194-228.

sphere of influence. It is a group of either family or friends who are known by the host or group leader.

Yet there is still another potential setting for evangelism. There is an opportunity for a recipient to attend a local church, perhaps by the invitation of a friend. While the recipient attends church, they hear the gospel message and have an opportunity during the call for invitation to accept Christ. This is what Robert Webber calls liturgical evangelism.[221] This type of evangelism should be included in the local church's list of evangelical resources, because one does not know how the Holy Spirit is going to move.

A plan for evangelism.

In developing a plan for evangelism, should it be developed, implemented, and then left alone? According to Robert Coleman, evangelistic plans are not fixed and are subject to variation.[222] He takes the position of evaluating a plan and making changes based on the results.[223] This takes on the risk of evaluating the plan from a human viewpoint devoid of God's intentions. Coleman does have positive intentions: the incorporation of new, bold approaches.[224] His justification is that "methods that were extremely popular a hundred years ago may have little appeal today."[225] His method for

---

[221] Robert E. Webber, *Liturgical Evangelism: Worship as Outreach and Nurture* (Harrisburg, PA: Morehouse Publishing, 1986), 1.

[222] Coleman, *The Master Plan of Evangelism,* 108.

[223] Ibid.

[224] Ibid.

[225] Coleman, *Evangelism in Perspective,* 42.

determining the effectivity of a method is based on results: "Old forms need to be periodically evaluated in light of their effectiveness. Unproductive policies and techniques should be discarded when a better way is found . . . not everything will get results."[226]

In contrast, James Logan cautioned a local church to watch out for what he calls "practical pragmatism."[227] This principle is based on using methods that get positive results as the sole factor in determining appropriate methods for evangelism. Does this intuitively sound like a secular approach? Logan's position is that this type of planning lacks a "theological conscience."[228] If believers are going to conduct evangelism, shouldn't they plan according to how the Spirit empowers them and in accordance with God's Word? This would involve a disciplined approach of church planning: considering God's Word and praying for methods to consider.

Another consideration in planning evangelism is to take into account the needs of the recipients. The local church should consider placing their believers into positions where they will ask a recipient the following question: "How can we be of help to you?"[229] This is related more to the focus of evangelism. We tend to think that evangelism is all about proclaiming the gospel to a recipient. But what is the view of the recipient? What are they thinking of when two people come knocking on their door? The

---

[226] Ibid.

[227] Logan, *Theology and Evangelism in the Wesleyan Heritage,* 13.

[228] Ibid.

[229] Hunter, *The Contagious Congregation*, 52.

perception of the recipient is centered more on what *they* think they need instead of what *others* think they need. So the key to the planning process is to segue the conversation toward their needs. In fact, at some point, the conversation could shift to the fact that we are all sinners, and the wages of our sin is eternal death (Romans 3:23; 6:23).

Visitations must be accomplished in an appropriate fashion. For example, a couple in Florida became disinterested when called upon during a visitation because the callers did not make them feel like Christians.[230] The callers had a message in mind that they were going to deliver, but they did not take into account the point of view of those being visited. On another occasion, a woman in Baltimore became disinterested because those visiting were obnoxious by overstaying their visit.[231] Here again, the viewpoint of those being called upon must be taken into account. The methodology for evangelism is not merely dispensing the gospel, but to listen and ascertain the recipient's viewpoint. Callers are there to listen to the recipients.[232] In order to effectively minister to others with the gospel, *the recipient's* setting must be taken into account.

How to start conversations and how to consider residents' needs are important for door-to-door visitations. But further preparation should be done before knocking on doors. Michael Green provided this strategy or list of goals when preparing for this ministry:[233]

---

[230] Richard Stoll Armstrong, *Service Evangelism* (Philadelphia, PA: The Westminster Press, 1979), 79-80.

[231] Ibid.

[232] Ibid., 81.

[233] Green, *Evangelism through the Local Church*, 540.

1. Establish a good relationship

2. Gather family information for use later on

3. Offer to pick up resident to attend a service or event

4. Speak about Christ

5. Offer to pray for family members or specific needs

6. Leave them with literature

It is important to write these down on a clipboard as reminders when performing visitations. These are key points to keep in mind before and during a conversation. We don't know what the residents will say or how the conversation will go, but keeping these goals in mind will allow believers to minister appropriately to each resident.

Group activities should be planned in a home or "neutral" location.[234] Some recipients may not feel comfortable going into a church for the first time. They are unfamiliar with: (1) the inside of the church, (2) the people, and (3) how the activities or church service is conducted. This type of angst may cause the recipient to feel reluctant to attend the church, even if invited by a friend. Ronald Runyon offered some suggestions on what activities recipients could be initially invited to:[235]

1. Evangelistic home Bible study

---

[234] Runyon, "Principles and Methods of Household Evangelism," 72-73.
[235] Ibid.

2. Evangelistic entertaining event (e.g. meal)

3. Local evangelistic function (e.g. concert)

4. Seasonal party (e.g. Christmas, Valentine's Day)

5. Christian film

6. Neighborhood block party

7. Craft class

Acts 2:46 indicates that the early Christians met in their homes. This gives credence to G.A. Getz's statement that "Christianity is supremely a household religion and is best propagated to households in family circles and in homes."[236] A local church may plan a series of outreach events, but the goal is to start a home group where the recipients feel comfortable.

We must explore the concept of crusade evangelism.[237] We previously noted that Christianity grew when early Christians met in their homes (Acts 2:46), but the Holy Spirit was previously poured out among three thousand souls on the day of Pentecost (Acts 2:1-41). We must be careful not to constrain the Spirit by just thinking about having home Bible studies, but we must prayerfully consider a city-wide evangelistic event.

---

[236] G.A. Getz, review of George W. Peters, *Saturation Evangelism* (Grand Rapids, MI: Zondervan Publishing House, 1970), *Bibliotheca Sacra* 128, no. 510 (April – June 1971), 153-154.
[237] Huston, *Crusade Evangelism and the Local Church,* 36-37.

The crusade involves the cooperation of at least several local churches. Planning committees are setup to handle functions such as a prayer team, a planning team, a logistics team, etc. In parallel with the planning functions, the churches collectively perform an intensive door-to-door visitation program where the gospel is presented and the recipients are invited to the crusade event. Dr. Roger Fredrikson (past president of American Baptist Churches) noted that when a crusade came to his city, more professions of faith were made in the six weeks prior to the crusade than during any other time of his ministry.[238]

Enlisting the help of other churches for any type of campaign should not be underestimated. A group of pastors from various churches in Indianapolis in 1913 agreed to conduct a three-day city-wide visitation program.[239] Volunteers from these churches went house-to-house throughout the city sharing the gospel. These pastors claimed that 20,000 new members were added across their congregations. In the following year, the Church Federation of St. Louis launched what they called the "One-to-Win-One" campaign.[240] The churches recruited volunteers to conduct a religious census to discover prospects among the local residents. These volunteers were trained by the pastors to visit and share the gospel with unbelievers. The volunteers asked the prospects to sign a pledge to join one of the participating churches. The pastors then visited those who signed pledges. The Federation claimed that over 10,000 new members joined the area

---

[238] Ibid.

[239] William G. McLoughlin, *Modern Revivalism* (New York, NY: Ronald Press, 1959), 456.

[240] Ibid.

churches as a result of the campaign. Are we surprised at such statistics? Do we believe

that God is able to perform such an activity no matter what the results? Are we willing to

plan and conduct a culture-specific program for our own congregations, enlisting the

guidance of the Holy Spirit and giving Christ the results?

Which method does the Holy Spirit utilize (crusades, evangelistic outreach events,

door-to-door visitations, etc.) for a local church? The answer, unequivocally, is *all* of

them. A believer, or group of believers, cannot predict exactly how the Spirit will work.

We must simply be servants performing our duty. Jesus told His disciples that their

response in doing the Lord's work should be: "We are unworthy servants; we have only

done our duty" (Luke 17:10).

Survey questions for evangelism.

How is personal communication established? The believer should show grace to

the recipient by not only asking questions, but responding gracefully to their answers.

Jerram Barrs suggested a method whereby the recipient is commended for their responses

to opening questions.[241] Sometimes it is helpful to first find out if the recipient is ready

for a conversation. Some probing questions could be the following:[242]

1. What is your religious heritage?

2. Has your heritage helped you answer the important questions you are asking

   in life?

---

[241] Barrs, *The Heart of Evangelism,* 207.

[242] Ken Hemphill, *Life Answers: Making Sense of Your World* (Nashville, TN: Lifeway Press, 1992), 13.

3. What are the questions you are asking?

Here is a list of survey questions:[243]

1. Do you believe in God?

2. Do you read the Bible?

3. Do you live in obedience to God's Laws?

4. Do you admire Christ?

5. Do you believe in afterlife and judgment?

D. James Kennedy offered this question for the recipient: "Do you know for sure that you have eternal life?"[244] Also, consider the following questions from Michael Green:[245]

1. Do you think there are any solid grounds for hope these days?

2. Do you think the Christian church has any real hope to hold out to people?

3. If you could meet Jesus Christ, would you want to?

Another method for asking questions is to reference the following acronym from Darrell Robinson:[246]

1. F – Family

2. I – Interests

---

[243] Ibid.

[244] Kennedy, *Evangelism Explosion,* 15.

[245] Green, *Evangelism through the Local Church*, 536.

[246] Darrell W. Robinson, *People Sharing Jesus* (Nashville, TN: Thomas Nelson Publishers, 1995), 58.

3. R – Religion

4. M – Message

Asking questions about a person's family is a great conversation starter. How many children do they have? What are their ages? Are they involved in any community activities? These questions also allow the believer to discover some areas where the local church can minister to the family. Interests are another important topic. Are they interested in sports? Do they enjoy doing house or yard work? (This can usually be spotted when walking up the front steps to the house.) The topic of religion is another good conversation starter. Do they believe in spiritual things? Are they currently attending a church? (This type of survey can lead into the sharing of a tract, which usually has good questions to segue into the gospel message.) All of these questions lead up to engaging the final topic – the Message. Have they heard of the message of Jesus Christ, and His sacrifice for our sins?

Perhaps one of the greatest survey questions is to ask a person how you can pray for them. Donald Whitney highlighted a technique whereby he asked this question and told the person that his church was having a special prayer service to pray for the requests of all the residents in the neighborhood.[247] He was astounded by the ease in which he could discuss spiritual issues with these people.

These are great questions to open up a conversation about the gospel after believers have introduced themselves and specified that they are genuinely concerned

---

[247] Donald S. Whitney, *Spiritual Disciplines for the Christian Life* (Colorado Springs, CO: NavPress, 1991), 109.

about the needs of the community. Once one of the above questions is posed, the recipient will respond with their answer. Believers should be quick to commend them for their admiration in this area.[248] Survey questions keep the recipients engaged in conversation, and commending them for their answers shows love and concern.

The above questions are appropriate because they do not assume that the believer knows anything about the recipient's spiritual beliefs. George Hunter offered an inductive method, which does take into account that the recipient has some spiritual beliefs:[249]

1. How has God helped you in the past?

2. What experiences have you had where you were helped to get through something and someone was guiding you?

This inductive method may be appropriate for conversations with friends or family, since the believer has some knowledge about the recipient's past history. This would be a preferred method, because it encourages the recipient to initiate conversation about God. Permission does not need to be obtained from the recipient to talk about their personal spiritual beliefs, because they are already providing the answers to the questions. This is a more advanced approach to the conversation because of the existing relationship between the believer and the recipient.

---

[248] Barrs, *The Heart of Evangelism,* 207.

[249] Hunter, *The Contagious Congregation,* 54.

Another method for addressing recipients is to provide support when they are experiencing a change in their lives. Stephen VanHorn suggested that a believer be aware of these potential changes in a recipient's life:[250]

1. Death

2. Divorce

3. Illness

4. Status change

These changes in life cause recipients to reflect on what is important in life. These thoughts allow one to shift their thinking away from the superficial, material things to the spiritual dimension, which allow them to be more open to the gospel.

Profile of the Current Study

This summary describes the shaping of this research with respect to the following questions which are reformatted from the hypotheses stated earlier:

1. What is the theology of NT evangelism?

2. What is the biblical mandate for NT evangelism?

3. What is the cultural setting for NT evangelism?

---

[250] Stephen VanHorn, "*Oikos* Evangelism and Church Growth," (M.A.B.S. Thesis, International Christian Graduate University, School of Theology, Arrowhead Springs, CA, 1981), addendum.

The Theology of NT Evangelism

Evangelism was a focal part both of Jesus' ministry as well as the disciples after Jesus' ascension with regards to the Church. God's perception of evangelism is that it falls under His calling and His grace. The proper perception of His calling is not from a human worldview, but rather from a divine viewpoint. Isaiah records God's viewpoint in Isaiah 55:8: "For my thoughts are not your thoughts, neither are your ways my ways." We have to recognize that He is the One who initiates the calling, and not a biblical leader. Consider this metaphor spoken by Jesus Christ: "You are the salt of the earth. But if the salt loses its saltiness, how can it be make salty again? It is no longer good for anything except to be thrown out and trampled underfoot" (Matthew 5:13). Therefore, considering the orthodoxy of evangelism, the Church is required by Christ to incorporate evangelism into its ministry.

The Biblical Mandate for NT Evangelism

The biblical mandate refers to what Scripture tells us about evangelism when it comes to orthopraxis. It encompasses the daily beliefs and actions a believer should make to employ evangelism properly. It order to be productive in God's eyes, a believer should "meditate on his [God's] law day and night. That person is like a tree planted by streams of water, which yields its fruit in season and whose leaf does not wither – whatever they do prospers" (Psalm 1:2-3). A believer also prepares for evangelism out of obedience to Christ. Paul had this to say about his obedience as he wrote to the Philippians, "I consider everything a loss because of the surpassing worth of knowing Christ Jesus my Lord, for whose sake I have lost all things. I consider them garbage, that I may gain Christ" (Philippians 3:8). Paul, here, is not distracted by those things which would interfere with his obedience to Christ. This is a key principle for the believer, since evangelism can only be accomplished through the aforementioned power and sufferings of Christ. Any distraction from the believer's obedience will compromise Christ's work through the believer. The impetus for this is a sacrificial heart. A believer must hold onto the things of this world lightly so that obedience is preserved. The sacrificial heart of a believer brings a person into Christ's presence out of obedience, while having a disdain for those things which attempt to distract the believer from the Lord Jesus Christ and His Word.

The local church was destined to exist to be an evangelistic camp for the local community. Evangelism is an essential part of the local church. This is not based on a relative assessment of how we sort out Scripture amongst ecclesiastical activities, but rather it involves the power of God, and is therefore, a divine function with divine appointments. If the Church is to accomplish the mission of Jesus Christ today, then it must discover Christ's true mission according to His word. Christ's mission is not just to congregate in the four walls of a building, but to warn the community regarding sin and eternal life. There is accountability for the Church to share the gospel according to Ezekiel 3. Does the Church realize this?

The Cultural Setting for NT Evangelism

Each local church is located in a unique setting as compared with other churches. Therefore, the cultural dynamics will be different. For example, we know that each believer that comes into a local church has different (unique) gifts. No two people are exactly alike, so the dynamics that result from a particular believer in a particular local church are unique. The collection of unique believers results in a unique local church. Therefore, we would expect that the outreach concerns and potential for that local church to be unique from any other local church.

It is the responsibility of each Christian, as well as the Church, to learn about evangelism and its importance in God's Kingdom and to make application from that learning. The basic definition of evangelism is the sharing of the good news that Jesus Christ sacrificed Himself on the cross for our sins so that the one who accepts this mercy and trusts Christ as their Lord now experiences new life. But what did Jesus Christ have in mind when He said "go and make disciples" in Matthew 28:19? If a recipient were to fall under this definition of evangelism, and thereby, become a believer in obedience to God's Word, they would recognize that Matthew 28:19 requires them to engage in evangelism. This is a cyclical process of new believers coming to Christ, and then out of obedience, sharing the gospel so that other recipients may also ask forgiveness for their sins and put their trust in Christ.

Chapter 3

Methodological Design

Design Overview

The research question restated is: What are the similarities and differences between churches in Southeastern Massachusetts and Rhode Island and the evangelism as practiced in the New Testament by Jesus Christ, His disciples, and the apostle Paul, and how can churches in Southeastern Massachusetts and Rhode Island focus more on New Testament evangelism?

This research included informal interviews conducted with biblical leaders to gather information on how churches in Southeastern Massachusetts and Rhode Island approach evangelism. The responses provided by the interviewees were used to substantiate certain claims made by this author. Since this research involved interviews with human subjects, it would normally be classified as a quantitative method since we are collecting some data from the interviewees that results in a yes or no answer. However, this research also falls into the qualitative domain, since some of the data must be interpreted as being sufficient enough to substantiate the claims being made by this author. This empirical research falls under the qualitative method involving a phenomenological study.[251] A phenomenological study seeks to gather data with the

---

[251] Paul D. Leedy and Jeanne Ellis Ormrod, *Practical Research: Planning and Design,* 9th ed. (Boston: Pearson, 2010), 141-142.

interviewee's perception in mind. The sample size for this type should be in the range of between five and twenty-five individuals.[252] This stage of the research was conducted as informal interviews (one to two hours in length) on a one-on-one basis.

Population

There are 648 churches in Rhode Island[253] and 857 churches in Southeastern Massachusetts as of this writing.[254] It would have been a difficult endeavor timewise to interview a biblical leader from each one of these churches. Perhaps this could be considered as a further study. Furthermore, verbal consent would have to be obtained, and it is unknown as to how many of these leaders would actually consent to such an interview.

Samples and Delimitations

This author selected biblical leaders which represent a cross-section of several denominations in Rhode Island and Southeastern Massachusetts. These leaders are respectable and deemed by this author as being honest and credible. This author has established a rapport with these leaders: one over the last year, one over twenty-five

---

[252] Ibid., 146.

[253] "Yellow Pages," Yahoo, accessed February 18, 2016, http://www.yellowpages.com/providence-ri/churches.

[254] "Yellow Pages," Yahoo, accessed February 18, 2016, http://www.yellowpages.com/search?search_terms=churches&geo_location_terms=Rehoboth%2C+MA.

years, and the remainder over several years. This author has earned the mutual respect of these leaders. They represent the following denominations and locations, respectively: (1) Southern Baptist, Rhode Island; (2) Independent Fundamental Baptist, Southeastern Massachusetts; (3) Greek Orthodox, Rhode Island; (4) Non-denominational (elder led), Massachusetts; and (5) Methodist, Rhode Island.

Limitations of Generalization

There are 1,505 churches representing the whole population of churches in Southeastern Massachusetts and Rhode Island as of this writing. The sample size chosen representing five churches is relatively small compared to the whole population. Each of the five churches, however, represented a different denomination. This contributed to the inferential statistical analysis below, since each sample is totally distinct and represents a different denomination. There is a possibility, however, that there could be new information from another sample taken from the whole population.

For the purposes of this study, sampling from the various denominations among the five churches showed contrasting views regarding evangelism. These contrasting views represented differences in theological perspectives. Nevertheless, the samples chosen were used to either substantiate or deny the research hypotheses made by this author.

The relatively small sample size compared to the large population resulted in an inferential statistical analysis.[255] We are interested in whether or not an observed result is by chance alone. This will factor into whether or not the research hypotheses made by this author are valid. If the observed result occurred by chance alone, then this phenomenon is called the null hypothesis (H_o).[256] If the observed result did not occur by chance, then we reject the null hypothesis. Here are the hypotheses put forth by this author:

1. Churches in Southeastern Massachusetts and Rhode Island are not following the biblical mandate for evangelism.

2. Most churches in Southeastern Massachusetts and Rhode Island do not understand the theology of New Testament evangelism.

3. The cultural setting for churches today in Southeastern Massachusetts and Rhode Island is vastly different than that of the Middle East 2000 years ago.

The significance factor (α) defines that a result did not occur by chance alone.[257] This threshold is 1-in-5 ($\alpha=0.2$), reflected by the sample size. Any sample set that is equal to or greater than the threshold is statistically significant and will reject the null

---

[255] Leedy and Ormrod, *Practical Research: Planning and Design,* 275.

[256] Ibid., 278.

[257] Ibid., 279.

hypothesis.[258] If this is the case, then the observed samples did not occur by chance and will substantiate the hypotheses made by this author.

Instrumentation

This author met with each interviewee separately, in a comfortable, relaxed, and fairly quiet setting. The questions listed in Appendix A (Interview Questions) were asked of each interviewee. This method of instrumentation was chosen since it yielded more in-depth information than static response methods.[259] This author made a separate file containing the list of questions, and recorded the interviewee's answers into this file on his PC. There was one file for each interviewee.

This author subdued any preconceived notions regarding the subject matter. He kept an open mind, taking the perspective of the interviewee as the responses were gathered and recorded. The goal for each interview was to focus on what that particular interviewee was saying (irrespective of how the responses agree or disagree with this author's initial hypotheses).

---

[258] Ibid.

[259] Sharan B. Merriam and Edwin L. Simpson, *A Guide to Research for Educators and Trainers of Adults,* 2nd ed. (Malabar, FL: Krieger Publishing Company, 2000), 71.

Interview Questions

The questions listed in Appendix A (Interview Questions) were developed to provide evidence for the author's hypotheses, which in turn, answered the research question. The interviewees were each separately interviewed to systematically gather their responses to the question listed in Appendix A. The interviewees had no knowledge of each other's participation or contributions to this research. The answers for each interviewee are posted in Appendix B (Responses to Interview Questions).

Chapter 4

Analysis of Findings

Since this research involved interviews with human subjects, it would normally be classified as a quantitative method since we collected some data from the interviewees that results in a yes or no answer. However, this research also falls into the qualitative domain, since some of the data must be interpreted as being sufficient enough to substantiate the claims being made by this author. This empirical research falls under the qualitative method involving a phenomenological study.[260]

Compilation Protocol

Quantitative Perspective

From a quantitative perspective, three of the interview questions resulted in a yes or no answer:

1. Does your denomination hold to any specific views regarding evangelism?

2. Does your denomination think that evangelism is important?

3. Do you think your immediate neighborhood is responsive to evangelism?

---

[260] Paul D. Leedy and Jeanne Ellis Ormrod, *Practical Research: Planning and Design,* 9th ed. (Boston: Pearson, 2010), 141-142.

These responses were tallied and illustrated as described in Table 1 and Figure 2 of Chapter 1. The purpose of these figures is to summarily answer whether or not churches are responding to evangelism today as put forth in the research question: What are the similarities and differences between churches in Southeastern Massachusetts and Rhode Island and the evangelism as practiced in the New Testament by Jesus Christ, His disciples, and the apostle Paul, and how can churches in Southeastern Massachusetts and Rhode Island focus more on New Testament evangelism?

Qualitative Perspective

For the qualitative perspective, the three hypotheses that support the research question are listed here with the interview questions from Appendix A as being subordinate to their respective hypothesis:

I. Churches in Southeastern Massachusetts and Rhode Island are not following the biblical mandate for evangelism.

    a. How would you define NT evangelism?

    b. Does your denomination hold to any specific views regarding evangelism?

    c. Does your denomination think that evangelism is important?

    d. What do you think are the major obstacles that your fellow church members have in regards to sharing Christ?

e. What do you think your church can do to increase church awareness regarding evangelism in the local neighborhood?

II.   Most churches in Southeastern Massachusetts and Rhode Island do not understand the theology of New Testament evangelism.

a. How would you define NT evangelism?

b. Which NT Scriptures do you think are applicable to evangelism?

III. The cultural setting for churches today in Southeastern Massachusetts and Rhode Island is vastly different than that of the Middle East 2000 years ago.

a. What techniques do you think are appropriate for NT evangelism?

b. What techniques does your denomination deem appropriate for NT evangelism?

c. What techniques on evangelism do you see as being applied in the NT?

d. Do you think your immediate neighborhood is responsive to evangelism? Why or why not?

e. What do you think are the major obstacles that local residents have in regards to accepting Christ?

The in-depth responses to these questions were tallied and illustrated in tables corresponding to their respective hypothesis (see Table 2 of Chapter 1 for a sample table). The purpose of these tables is to show what the similarities and differences are

between various denominations today regarding the research question. Are the responses

for each phenomenon similar enough so that we can make a summarized answer and then

compare it to the evangelism as practiced in the NT by Jesus Christ, His disciples, and the

apostle Paul?

Findings and Displays

Quantitative Perspective

From a quantitative perspective, the three interview questions resulting in a yes or

no answer were tabulated in Table 8. The information for this table is contained in

Appendix B (Responses to Interview Questions).

Table 8. Number of denominations responding to evangelism (responses from interviews)

Question	Number of Denominations Responding in the Affirmative
Does your denomination hold to any specific views regarding evangelism?	5
Does your denomination think that evangelism is important?	3
Do you think that your immediate neighborhood is responsive to evangelism?	0

These responses were extrapolated into the graph in Figure 3.

New Testament Evangelism

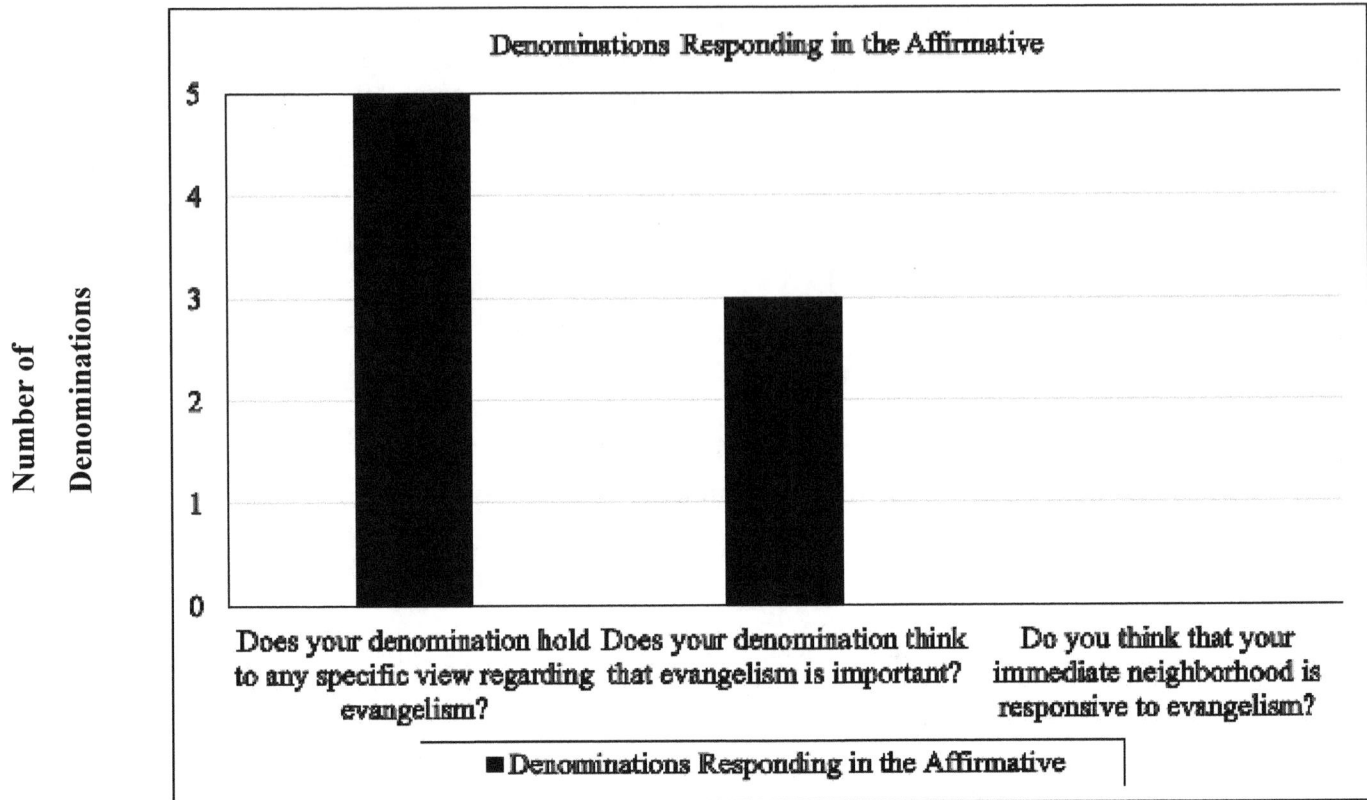

Figure 3. Denominations responding in the affirmative (actual responses)

Qualitative Perspective

From a qualitative perspective, the remaining responses to the interview questions are given in Tables 9 through 11. The information for these tables is contained in Appendix B (Reponses to Interview Questions). These tables have a summarized response for each question. The summarized responses from each denomination are shown side-by-side for contrast. Table 9 has the responses regarding the theological basis for evangelism, Table 10 records those responses regarding the biblical mandate for evangelism, and Table 11 stores the responses pertaining to the cultural setting and

techniques for evangelism.

Table 9. Responses regarding the theological basis for evangelism

Response	SB	IFB	Greek Orthodox	Methodist	Non-denominational
Definition of NT evangelism	Great Commission; conversion, discipleship, multiplication	Great Commission; good news of why Christ came	Teaching Christian values and faith in God	Sending out believers so that others would receive forgiveness & faith	Speak to others about Christ & being light to others
NT Scriptures applicable to NT evangelism	Math 5, 28:18-20; John 14:6, 3:16; Acts 4:12; Romans 3:23, 6:23, 5:8, 10:11-12; Rev 20:11-15	John 3, 4; Acts 1:8; 2 Tim 4; Hebrews 10:3, 10:23	Math 25	Romans 8:1; 1 Cor 1:18, 2:6; 1 Tim 4:11-13	Math 5:14-16, 28:19-20; Mark 8:35, 16:15; John 13:35; Acts 1:8, 13:47, 20:24; Rom 1:16, 10:17; 1 Cor 2:2, 15:1-2; Titus 2:1; 1 Peter 3:15

Table 10. Responses regarding the biblical mandate for evangelism

Response	SB	IFB	Greek Orthodox	Methodist	Non-denominational
Denom. views regarding evangelism	Great Commission; church planting	Missions comm. sends out two-by-two to other people	Share love and news of Christ with intention of recipient forming personal relationship with Christ	Street evangelism; household Bible studies	Live life of gospel to be effective
Obstacles fellow members have sharing Christ	Fear of rejection; perception of sharing gospel is difficult; interference from other religions	Perception of sharing gospel is difficult	Fear of other people; focus within parish; new people either born into or married into parish	Reluctance to change from not sharing to sharing Christ; comfortable just knowing about Christ	Too comfortable in local church; afraid do not know Scripture enough & are not trained about spreading gospel
Church awareness regarding evangelism	Keep talking about it corporately and personally concerning what Christ has done for them & concerning Great White Throne seat of judgment	Preach from pulpit; get people excited about sharing Christ; train them; encourage Scripture memory to assist in sharing	Articulate similarities & differences of Greek Orthodoxy (neither Catholic nor Protestant)	Preach from pulpit; invite them to consider specific gifts; assign small groups (food pantry, door-to-door); increase budget for evangelism	Block party with tracts to share faith; games for kids; door-to-door invitation for Resurrection Day service; use food program to increase awareness

New Testament Evangelism

Table 11. Responses regarding the cultural setting and techniques for evangelism

Response	SB	IFB	Greek Orthodox	Methodist	Non-denominational
Techniques your *denom.* deems appropriate for NT evangelism	Be prepared to share gospel in every phase of life	Pulpit: message & invitation	Priest involved with RI group of leaders; prayer	Food pantries, community gardens, missionary trips, UMCOR	Kids program; NH ministry; missions; Bible translators, food program
Techniques *you* deem appropriate for NT evangelism	Be prepared to share gospel in every phase of life	Need to be Spirit-filled; get to know person	Open discussion with those in prison	Personal sharing, small groups, street preaching	Personal sharing; door-to-door
Techniques for evangelism as being applied in NT	John 4; Acts 17; street preaching; engaging with people	Math 10; Paul by personal sharing	Teachings from Christ and writers of epistles	Acts 26; sharing resources; healings	Spirit-filled; boldness; parables; preaching
Neighborhood responsive to evangelism (why/why not)	Negative view Church & Christianity	People are caught up in the world	Existing presuppositions; already attending church; uncomfortable with somebody visiting at door	Existing presuppositions	People are too comfortable; consider Christians weird
Major obstacles residents have towards accepting Christ	Our region least biblically-literate	Hard to do	People do not see need or are not interested	Sin; existing presuppositions	Do not want to change (have to give up something)

Evaluation of the Research Design

The eleven interview questions developed for the interview process take into account the theological, denominational, and personal viewpoints of the interviewees. These questions, however, may not be comprehensive enough to either substantiate or disapprove the claims made by this author.

There are five denominations represented by this interview process (one for each interviewee). Is this enough evidence for the author to substantiate claims regarding *all* Christian churches in Southeastern Massachusetts and Rhode Island? This is an apparent weakness in this methodology since not all denominations in this area are accounted for.

The biblical leaders selected as interviewees are pastors, elders, or ministry leaders. They are considered to be knowledgeable regarding the biblical basis for evangelism. They are also knowledgeable about their denomination's involvement in evangelism, having been affiliated with their respective denominations for over twenty years. These are assumptions, however, based on the perception of this author.

The objective responses of the interviewees is a strength of this methodology. The claims made by this author were substantiated by the responses from these biblical leaders, representing churches in Southeastern Massachusetts and Rhode Island.

The biblical leaders interviewed may not have a perspective that matches that of their respective local neighborhoods. They may not have conducted surveys to determine an accurate perspective from the residents' point of view.

The claims made by this author were substantiated both quantitatively and qualitatively. Obtaining yes or no answers from the interviewees answered some questions, but the in-depth responses provide more conclusive evidence to substantiate or prove otherwise this author's claims.

It may appear that a sample size of five interviewees is too small among a total population size of 1,505 churches in Southeastern Massachusetts and Rhode Island, although Leedy and Ormrod have established a sample size of between five and twenty-five individuals.[261] The sample size of five results in a significance factor of $\alpha=0.2$. This heightened factor results in a greater chance (compared to larger sample sizes) that this author may incorrectly reject the null hypothesis (that the author's claims occurred by chance) resulting in a Type I error.[262]

---

[261] Leedy and Ormrod, *Practical Research: Planning and Design,* 141-142.
[262] Ibid., 279.

Chapter 5

Conclusions

Since this research involved interviews with human subjects, it would normally be classified as a quantitative method since we are collecting some data from the interviewees that results in a yes or no answer. However, this research also falls into the qualitative domain, since some of the data must be interpreted as being sufficient enough to substantiate the claims being made by this author. This empirical research falls under the qualitative method involving a phenomenological study.[263]

Applied Research Purpose Statement

This research was performed to determine how effective Southeastern Massachusetts and Rhode Island churches are at practicing evangelism in their local areas. Are these churches practicing evangelism according to the way that Jesus Christ and His disciples practiced it? This research also uncovered how these churches can be more focused on evangelism. This is important because the results of evangelism will, from God's point of view, determine whether or not people have a relationship with Jesus Christ and subsequently eternal life. There are eternal ramifications at stake here.

---

[263] Paul D. Leedy and Jeanne Ellis Ormrod, *Practical Research: Planning and Design,* 9th ed. (Boston: Pearson, 2010), 141-142.

Implications of Findings

A summary of the research findings from the chapter on Literature Review as

well as responses from the interviewees are provided here. These findings have an impact

on the beliefs, theories, and practices on the topic of evangelism. The interview responses

are also correlated here to form an objective biblical and literary viewpoint. This

viewpoint will then be used in the Applications of Findings section to either substantiate

or disprove the hypotheses made by this author.

The Definition of Evangelism

John Stott presented a shortened definition of evangelism. He defined it as "the

announcement of the good news, irrespective of the results."[264] Stott's definition claimed

that evangelism is the presentation of the gospel alone.[265] Certainly, Stott was providing

room for the recipient's response. Not every person who listens to a gospel presentation,

however, has a conversion experience. Stott included this condition in his definition to

allow both a conversion type of response on the part of the recipient, and a non-

conversion response.

The definition provided by J.D. Douglas concurs with that provided by John Stott.

Douglas claimed that "to evangelize is to spread the good news that Jesus Christ died for

---

[264] John Stott, *Christian Mission in the Modern World* (Downers Grove, IL: InterVarsity Press, 1975), 35.

[265] In the Literature Review, we uncovered other authors who defined evangelism as either a conversion experience (Coleman) or a life-long process of obedience to God's Word (Hunter).

our sins and was raised from the dead according to the Scriptures, and that as the reigning

Lord he now offers the forgiveness of sins and the liberating gift of the Spirit to all who

repent and believe."[266] There is nothing mentioned here regarding the recipients response

to the gospel message. It is simply a communication to the recipient(s). From Ephesians

4:11, the word "evangelists" (*euangelistes*) means the "one who declares good news."[267]

Therefore, the definition supplied by both Stott and Douglas is consistent with

that of Ephesians 4:11. From Table 9, four of the five interviewees indicated that

evangelism involves speaking to others outside of the church body about Christ

(including references to the Great Commission in Matthew 28). The fifth interviewee

considered evangelism as "teaching Christian values." This is outside of the bounds of

the Scriptural definition. This viewpoint is construed as teaching within the church body.

One of the interviewees even considered evangelism as encompassing conversion,

discipleship, and multiplication. This too is outside of the bounds of the Scriptural

definition.

Only two of the interviewees from the interview process made explicit reference

to Matthew 5 (being salt and light) and Matthew 28 (the Great Commission). Another

interviewee made reference to the conversation between Jesus and the Samaritan woman

in John 4. Still another interviewee, in commenting about the sharing of the gospel,

---

[266] J.D. Douglas, ed., *Let the Earth Hear His Voice* (Minneapolis, MN: World Wide Publications, 1975), in *Planning Strategies for World Evangelization,* Edward R. Dayton and David A. Frazier (Grand Rapids, MI: William B. Eerdmans Publishing Company, 1990), 51.

[267] Spiros Zodhiates and Warren Baker, eds., *Hebrew-Greek Key Word Study Bible: Key Insights into God's Word* (Chattanooga, TN: AMG Publishers, 1996), 1628.

referenced 1 Corinthians 1:18 which mentions that the message of the cross is the power of God. Interesting enough, the interviewee who defined evangelism as teaching Christian values pointed to the parable of the ten virgins in Matthew 25. This parable urges people to be prepared for the second coming of Christ.

The Importance of Evangelism

From a holistic perspective, the Church is commissioned by Christ to proclaim the gospel so that the complete number of Gentiles will enter the promise of eternity with Christ. Paul proclaimed in Romans 11:25 that Israel experienced a hardening until the full number of Gentiles have entered the Church. "Full number" (*pleroma*) is defined as "complete number."[268] That is, there is a specific quantity of believers that Christ is bringing into His Church before He returns. Because God is omniscient, He already foreknows and has foreordained those who will enter His Church.[269] The initial process by which He brings souls into His Church is evangelism.

John Stott considered evangelism as an essential part of the Church's mission, but it is not the primary mission.[270] In his lecture, Stott argued that the Great Commission ("Go and make disciples of all nations . . ." - Matthew 28:16-20) is distinct from the

---

[268] Ibid., 1663.

[269] Charles F. Pfeiffer and Everett F. Harrison, eds., *The Wycliffe Bible Commentary* (Chicago, IL: Moody Press, 1962), 1218.

[270] John R.W. Stott, "The Nature of Biblical Evangelism" (lecture, Palais de Beaulieu, Lausanne, Switzerland, July 16, 1974).

Great Commandment ("Love the Lord your God . . ." – Matthew 22:37-39).[271] Hence,

Stott considers that the primary mission of the Church is to worship God, but evangelism

is still an essential part. Figure 3, however, shows that only three out of the five

interviewees from the interview process considered evangelism as being important.

The Audience for Evangelism

The geographical scope of evangelism is everywhere.[272] Therefore, there are no

limitations as to where the gospel can be spread; this could be the local neighborhood, the

city, the country, as well as other countries. Jesus was specific about this when He said,

"But you will receive power when the Holy Spirit comes on you; and you will be my

witnesses in Jerusalem, and in all Judea and Samaria, and to the ends of the earth" (Acts

1:8). This is coupled with the strata within a local community. Businesses as well as

residents should be contacted.[273] The two types of people available in a local community

are the people who live there and the people who work there.

The results in Figure 3, however, indicate that all the interviewees from the

interview process did *not* think that their immediate neighborhood is responsive to

evangelism. From Table 11, the reasons why they perceived that these people are not

responsive are:

---

[271] Ibid.

[272] Sterling W. Huston, *Crusade Evangelism and the Local Church* (Minneapolis, MN: World Wide Publications, 1984), 35.

[273] C.E. Autrey, *Evangelism in the Acts* (Grand Rapids, MI: Zondervan, 1964), 82.

1. They have a negative view of the Church and Christianity

2. They are caught up in the world

3. They are too comfortable

4. They have existing presuppositions about spiritual things

The interviewees also provided what they considered as the major obstacles that the local residents have towards accepting Christ:

1. They do not want to change

2. They do not see the need

3. Sin

4. Our region is the least biblically-literate

Training for Evangelism

In order to comply with the Great Commission, pastors (as leaders) are responsible for motivating their congregations to evangelize.[274] Someone has to take the responsibility for performing this function, and if the pastors don't, who will? Pastors act as models for shaping the culture of their congregations. How is the culture of their congregation shaped? Are they more concerned about church programs than lost souls?

---

[274] Donald A. McGavran, *Effective Evangelism: A Theological Mandate* (Phillipsburg, NJ: Presbyterian & Reformed Publishing Company, 1988), 154.

What would Jesus think of our pastors as models? Donald McGavran had this to say

about a pastor's responsibility to motivate their congregation to evangelize:[275]

> Some pastors have special gifts in evangelism. Many do not. But all pastors have
> the responsibility to facilitate evangelism in and through their congregations.
> Pastoral leadership in evangelism extends from the pulpit and classroom to the
> people in the pew who are moved to action by the Word and the Spirit and
> encouraged by the pastor's interest and example.

This type of leadership from the pulpit and the classroom extends from the

personal lives and behaviors of pastors. Pastors are the models for their congregations.

Calvin Ratz (et. al.) observed that "It's been said, 'a student learns what his teacher

knows, but a disciple becomes what his master is.' My people will not become what I say

they should be; they'll become what they see is important in my life. And that's true with

evangelism."[276] This is a striking comment, since pastors preach weekly to their

congregations about how to apply Scripture to one's personal life. Do members act on

what the pastor preaches, or do they model their lives after what they perceive is the

lifestyle of their pastor? Certainly people will listen to sermons, but at the same time,

they are observing how the pastor lives and what they consider important. How pastors

prioritize their lives will certainly impact how the members prioritize their lives.

Pastors do set an example and should have a positive attitude in reaching out to

the unchurched. Eventually, reaching out to those outside the church will result in growth

inside the church. Most pastors, however, desire growth if it does not affect the *status quo*

---

[275] Ibid.

[276] Calvin Ratz, Frank Tillapaugh, and Myron Ausburger, *Mastering Outreach & Evangelism* (Portland, OR: Multnomah, 1990), 26.

of the church.[277] Ben Johnson noted that "resistance to a change of style and composition and a refusal to share power block sustained growth."[278] This is not a straight-forward manner, but pastors must accept dynamic changes within the leadership and within the culture of the congregation. This will likely include sharing power. It is a humbling experience for a pastor to accept this. It might be worthwhile for the pastor to pray and reflect on 1 Corinthians 13:4: "Love . . . does not envy . . . it is not proud."

When it comes to training for evangelism, pastors need a proper perspective. They should be training members to evangelize rather than evangelizing themselves.[279] Roy Fish and J.E. Conant stated that even evangelists should not be the only ones doing the work: "An evangelist is not to go to a field and reap the harvest for the church while they look on. He is to lead, instruct, and direct the harvesters as they go out into the field and gather in the harvest themselves."[280] Unfortunately, the statistics do not indicate that pastors are training their members. Only 3-4% of pastors take their members out to evangelize and only 1½% of the members in a church body actually evangelize themselves.[281] D. James Kennedy points to the Acts 8 as the presupposition for why pastors should train their members.[282] After the stoning of Stephen, Luke indicated that

---

[277] Ben Johnson, *Evangelism Primer* (Atlanta, GA: John Knox Press, 1983), 70.

[278] Ibid.

[279] D. James Kennedy, *Evangelism Explosion* (London: Coverdale House Publishers, 1970), 6.

[280] Roy J. Fish and J.B. Conant, *Every Member Evangelism for Today* (New York, NY: Harper and Row Publishers, 1922), 16.

[281] D. James Kennedy, *Evangelism Explosion* (London: Coverdale House Publishers, 1970), 7.

[282] Ibid., 6.

"A great persecution broke out against the church in Jerusalem, and *all except the apostles* [italics mine] were scattered throughout Judea and Samaria" (Acts 8:1). The phrase, "*all except the apostles*," refers to the believers rather than the apostles. Acts 8:4 then follows with, "Those who had been scattered preached the word wherever they went." One definition of a disciple is not just an unbeliever coming to Christ, but a believer who is trained to spread the gospel so that an unbeliever can also come to Christ. This is a spiritual replication that defines what Jesus commanded in Matthew 28:19, when He said, "go and make disciples."

Michael Green provided a solid approach to help pastors mobilize their congregations for evangelism:[283]

1. Gain a passion for evangelism

2. Teach about it

3. Model it

4. Revive worship

5. Build up a team of committed volunteers

6. Generate unity within the team and the staff

7. Teach about spiritual weapons – prayer, Word, Holy Spirit, holiness, love

---

[283] Michael Green, *Evangelism through the Local Church* (Nashville, TN: Thomas Nelson Publishers, 1990), 414-415.

Green's approach is a structured, well-thought plan to promoting evangelism within the local church. Evangelism is not just recruiting a few volunteers and then proceed to visit households, but rather, it is a well-conceived, prayerful process. Cultivating a passion within the congregation takes time. In fact, it is very similar to the process of sanctification in a believer. In sanctification, believers grow in faith over a period of time by subjecting themselves to a number of opportunities for growth: (1) personal prayer and study of God's Word, (2) teaching (*didache*), (3) preaching (*kerygma*), (4) fellowship (*koinonia*), and (5) service (*diaconia*). Green's seven-step process is intended to "groom" volunteers over time to engage in evangelism.

The Setting for Evangelism

The generation of recipients must be taken into account. There are obviously various generations of recipients in our society, but there is a specific focus on the next generation. Who will be the Christian witnesses for the next generation? Christianity has endured and grown over the last two millennia, but are we to expect that growth to continue in the future? George Barna expressed this concern regarding the Bridgers (people born between 1977 and 1994):[284]

> The Bridgers are the first generation of Americans to be raised without the cultural presupposition that they would become Christians or explore Christianity. Many of the Bridgers take a smorgasbord approach to religion. They take the elements of each religion that make them most comfortable. They may even call themselves "Christians," but the term is used generically.

---

[284] George Barna, *Generation Next* (Ventura, CA: Regal, 1995), 74-75.

This is a very tenuous situation for this generation. No longer is Christianity systematically imposed or even taught to the next generation. Nevertheless, this is the setting that evangelists are exposed to today.

In a similar fashion in John 4:10-13, the Samaritan woman (being half Jew, half Gentile) did not immediately recognize the opportunity of having faith in Christ. Jesus said to her, "If you knew the gift of God and who it is that asks you for a drink, you would have asked him and he would have given you living water." To this she replied, "Sir, you have nothing to draw with and the well is deep. Where can you get this living water? Are you greater than our father Jacob, who gave us the well and drank from it himself, as did also his sons and his livestock?" Jesus then said, "Everyone who drinks this water will be thirsty again, but whoever drinks the water I give them will never thirst. Indeed, the water I give them will become in them a spring of water welling up to eternal life." Later in verse 25, the woman said, "I know that Messiah (called Christ) is coming. When he comes, he will explain everything to us." This points to the awareness of the prophecy by first century Jews and Gentiles, but not the immediate realization of Christ's presence. Our next generation faces a similar dilemma, they are not aware of the gospel message of Jesus Christ.

A Believer's Response to Evangelism

This may be a daunting statement to some, but according to Donald McGavran, a sign of spiritual renewal in any believer's heart is a passion for the lost.[285] He continued by indicating that one's own spiritual renewal, in fact, is proportional to one's response to the call for evangelism. The foundation for a relationship in Christ is a person's willingness to share the gospel:[286]

> No one can be *fully* biblically sound and spiritually renewed without being tremendously concerned about the multitudes of unreached men and women and, indeed, of unreached segments of society. It is impossible for anybody to be really in Christ, really full of the *Holy Spirit* [italics mine], without doing what the 120 did on the day of Pentecost. They rushed out and told everyone they met about Jesus and urged them to become his followers.

Would local congregations agree with McGavran? Have those who have ushered the isles of church pews for decades singing God's hymns acknowledge this? The Scripture in Acts 2:1-41 certainly appears to support McGavran's claim. The 120 were "filled with the Holy Spirit" (verse 4). The *Holy Spirit* used this opportunity to speak through Peter as he shared the gospel of Christ to those listening (verses 14-36). This proclamation of Christ led to the conversion (by the *Holy Spirit*) of over three thousand believers. We need to be honest with ourselves. Is our ministry a result of *our* participation with Christ, or is it a result of what the *Holy Spirit* is doing through us?

---

[285] McGavran, *Effective Evangelism,* 37.

[286] Ibid.

New Testament Evangelism

Bailey Smith encouraged believers to make evangelism central to their ministry.[287] If evangelism is viewed as something that a believer "does," then it becomes peripheral to what they are doing. It needs to be part of a believer's life. The following are some excuses for not doing evangelism, but they also serve as a check as to whether or not evangelism is incorporated into one's ministry:

1. Perform discipleship instead

2. Pursue "deeper life"

3. Too busy

4. Cultivating lost friends, but not sharing the gospel

Sharing the gospel should be part of a believer's ministry, without excuse. Jesus said, "If anyone is ashamed of me and my words in this adulterous and sinful generation, the Son of Man will be ashamed of them when he comes in his Father's glory with the holy angels" (Mark 8:38).

---

[287] Douglas M. Cecil, review of Bailey E. Smith, *Real Evangelism* (Nashville, TN: Word Publishing, 1999), *Bibliotheca Sacra* 157, no. 628 (October – December 2000), 505.

A Local Church's Response to Evangelism

Each of the seven churches in Revelation 2-3 were commended for their work, but were also rebuked for areas where they fell short in accomplishing Christ's work according to God's Word. The interface between Christ and the world was (and still is) through the Church. Colossians 1:24 provides us with the metaphor that Christ's body is the Church. Since Christ not only holds the keys to death and hades in Revelation 1:18 but also manages the book containing the names of those who will have eternal life (Revelation 20:11), it is therefore necessary for His Body (the Church) to share the good news of Christ with a world of recipients who are in danger of eternal death!

Evangelism was a focal part both of Jesus' ministry as well as the disciples after Jesus' ascension with regards to the Church. God's perception of evangelism is that it falls under His calling and His grace. The proper perception of His calling is not from a human worldview, but rather from a divine viewpoint. Therefore, considering the orthodoxy of evangelism, the Church is required by Christ to incorporate evangelism into its ministry.

The account in Luke 10:1-24 describes the commissioning of seventy-two believers to go out into "every town and place where he [Jesus] was about to go" (verse 1). The main focus is not whether this is personal evangelism, door-to-door evangelism, or world evangelism, but rather, the focus is on the "harvest" or need itself. In verse 2, Jesus explained that "The harvest is plentiful, but the workers are few. Ask the Lord of the harvest, therefore, to send out workers into his harvest field." Here we see the unique need of sharing Christ from God's point of view. Which point of view does the Church take today – Christ's or their own?

This missional work for the local church is to "create a community of Kingdom people."[288] If we reference Matthew 28 which specifies the making of disciples, we must assert that this process of making disciples begins with a conversion of the heart. The conversion of the heart, however, is based on the sharing of the gospel, or evangelism. The Kingdom perspective, therefore, is for the local church to be effective in evangelism in order to provide the gospel message.

One method of incorporating evangelism is to have an evangelistic group within the local church focused on outreach.[289] This group would not only operate in obedience to God's Word, but would operate in a pragmatic fashion: "Let the ardent Christians form missionary groups of evangelistic bands that will meet once a week or once a month to make sure that 'our congregation does win the lost in our community and give birth to daughter congregations at home and abroad.'"[290] Thus, the incorporation of evangelism leads to Church growth. This is not just necessarily a constant monitoring of numbers of believers in each congregation, but a realization that the overall Church is growing according to Christ's plan.

The denominational views as indicated by the interviewees from the interview process (Table 10) varied greatly regarding evangelism:

---

[288] Ben Campbell Johnson, *Rethinking Evangelism* (Philadelphia, PA: The Westminster Press, 1987), 121.
[289] McGavran, *Effective Evangelism,* 46.
[290] Ibid.

1. Great Commission and church planting

2. Sending out two believers by the Missions committee

3. Share the love and news of Christ

4. Street evangelism and household Bible studies

5. Live the life of the gospel

The interviewees also indicated the following obstacles that their fellow members have about sharing Christ:

1. Sharing the gospel is too difficult

2. They have a fear of other people

3. They are too comfortable in their church

When asked what their church could do to increase church awareness regarding evangelism in the local neighborhood, most of the interviewees responded with preaching from the pulpit. One interviewee suggested block parties and using the food program to increase awareness.

Evangelism versus the Social Gospel

Bock and Del Rosario claimed that evangelism and the social gospel should be "wedded together."[291] Jesus indicated that evangelism and the social gospel go together when He said, "I have testimony weightier than that of John. For the works that the Father has given me to finish – the very works that I am doing – testify that the Father has sent me" (John 5:36). He demonstrated this in Luke 4 when He spoke the Word from Isaiah 58 and 61 and then said, "The Lord has anointed me to release the captives." Then in Capernaum, He met the needs of the people. John Stott put it this way:[292]

> Although reconciliation with man is not reconciliation with God, nor is social action evangelism, nor is political liberation salvation, nevertheless we affirm that evangelism and socio-political involvement are both part of our Christian duty. For both are necessary expressions of our doctrines of God and man, our love for our neighbor and our obedience to Jesus Christ.

Believers must obtain an integrated focus of both evangelism and the social gospel in order to minister effectively. The two must be integrated together.

We can also look to evangelical leaders to see how they modeled the weaving of the social gospel and evangelism together. Some of the great evangelical leaders took note of the conditions in slum areas and responded to the physical needs of those living in those areas. Leaders such as F.B. Meyer, John Jowett, Charles Spurgeon, and T. deWitt

---

[291] Darrell L. Bock and Mike Del Rosario, "The Table Briefing: Tone and Truth in Cultural Engagement," *Bibliotheca Sacra* 173 (January – March, 2016), 98.

[292] John Stott, *The Lausanne Covenant: An Exposition and Commentary* (Minneapolis, MN: World Wide Publications, 1975), 20.

Talmage established gospel missions, employment bureaus, orphanages, and other organizations to meet the needs of these people.[293]

If evangelism is performed the way Jesus intended, we must come to the conclusion that it will result in social concern. We can look no further than the model Jesus established in Matthew 9 when he ministered to those on the hillside who were ostracized from society. He had a concern for both their physical and their spiritual needs when He said, "The harvest is plentiful but the workers are few. Ask the Lord of the harvest, therefore, to send out more workers into His harvest field" (Matthew 9:37-38). We also realize from John 4 that social concern can be a bridge to evangelism. In this passage, Jesus conversed with a Samaritan woman about thirst. This led to the sharing of Himself (the gospel) to her, to which she put her faith and trust in Him. We also note from Mark 10:46-52, that the blind Bartimaeus called upon Jesus: "Jesus, Son of David, have mercy on me!" Jesus asked what He could do for him, and the man indicated that he wanted to see. Jesus healed him, and said to him, "Go, your faith has healed you." How about the paralyzed man who was lowered in a stretcher from a roof because of the crowds. His determination and faith in Christ resulted in this statement from Jesus: "Friend, your sins are forgiven" (Luke 5:20). Jesus later instructed the paralyzed man in verse 24 to take his mat and go home. These examples demonstrate that social concern or social gospel is not void of evangelism, but works in tandem with it.

----

[293] David O. Moberg, *The Great Reversal: Evangelism and Social Concern*, rev. ed. (Philadelphia, PA: J.B. Lippincott Company, 1977), 28-29.

Conducting Outreach

Richard Armstrong worked extensively with an outreach program at the Presbyterian Church of Philadelphia in the 1950's and 1960's. From his experience, each church should have its own outreach program.[294] Each local church is located in a unique setting as compared with other churches. Therefore, the cultural dynamics will be different. We know that each believer that comes into a local church has different (unique) gifts. No two people are exactly alike, so the dynamics that result from a particular believer in a particular local church are unique. The collection of unique believers in a local church results in a unique local church. Therefore, we would expect that the outreach concerns and potential for that local church to be unique from any other local church.

The planning of outreach needs to take into consideration that the believers in the local church must go out and meet the non-believers in their setting. Ronald Runyon called this effort "community-centered" rather than "church-centered."[295] His premise was that recipients are more comfortable in their setting rather than a church setting. It is one thing for them to have to cross the spiritual threshold of a new life in Christ, but it is quite another when they have to cross the physical threshold of entering a building where they do not know anyone. This gives the recipient an opportunity to focus on Christ,

---

[294] Richard Stoll Armstrong, *Service Evangelism* (Philadelphia, PA: The Westminster Press, 1979), 178.

[295] Ronald D. Runyon, "Principles and Methods of Household Evangelism," *Bibliotheca Sacra* 142, no. 565 (January-March 1985), 70.

rather than being concerned about being recruited into a church.[296] Runyon is more focused on what he called "household evangelism"[297], a term he ascribed to sharing the gospel and helping new converts in their homes rather than in a church building.

Which method should a local church consider for outreach? Again, that comes back to the concept that outreach is conducted in concert with the Holy Spirit, and not just human wisdom from human authors. From this perspective, each local church is unique with its believers, their spiritual maturity level, and the unique community setting that they work in. The Spirit then empowers each local church in their unique setting.

A Plan for Evangelism

How to start conversations and how to consider residents' needs are important for door-to-door visitations. But further preparation should be done before knocking on doors. Michael Green provided this strategy or list of goals when preparing for these visitations:[298]

1. Establish a good relationship

2. Gather family information for use later on

3. Offer to pick up resident to attend a service or event

---

[296] Ibid.

[297] Ibid.

[298] Michael Green, *Evangelism through the Local Church* (Nashville, TN: Thomas Nelson Publishers, 1990), 540.

4. Speak about Christ

5. Offer to pray for family members or specific needs

6. Leave them with literature

It is important to write these down on a clipboard as reminders when performing visitations. These are key points to keep in mind before and during a conversation. We don't know what the residents will say or how the conversation will go, but keeping these goals in mind will allow believers to minister appropriately to each resident.

Group activities should be planned in a home or "neutral" location.[299] Some recipients may not feel comfortable going into a church for the first time. They are unfamiliar with the inside of the church, the people, and how the activities or church service is conducted. This type of angst may cause the recipient to feel reluctant to attend the church, even if invited by a friend. Ronald Runyon offered some suggestions on what activities recipients could be initially invited to:[300]

1. Evangelistic home Bible study

2. Evangelistic entertaining event (e.g. meal)

3. Local evangelistic function (e.g. concert)

4. Seasonal party (e.g. Christmas, Valentine's Day)

---

[299] Ronald D. Runyon, "Principles and Methods of Household Evangelism," *Bibliotheca Sacra* 142, no. 565 (January-March 1985), 72-73.

[300] Ibid.

5. Christian film

6. Neighborhood block party

7. Craft class

Acts 2:46 indicates that the early Christians met in their homes. This gives credence to G.A. Getz's statement that "Christianity is supremely a household religion and is best propagated to households in family circles and in homes."[301] A local church may plan a series of outreach events, but the goal is to start a home group where the recipients feel comfortable, possibly in one of their homes.

The interviewees from the interview process made these observations regarding techniques for evangelism as being applied in the NT (Table 11):

1. John 4 (Jesus' conversation with the Samaritan woman)

2. Matthew 10 (Jesus' commissioning of the disciples)

3. Acts 26 (Paul's defense before King Agrippa)

4. Teachings from Christ and the writers of the epistles

5. Spirit-filled, bold preaching

Regarding techniques that the interviewees considered appropriate for NT evangelism from their *denominational* perspective, they noted:

---

[301] G.A. Getz, review of George W. Peters, *Saturation Evangelism* (Grand Rapids, MI: Zondervan Publishing House, 1970), *Bibliotheca Sacra* 128, no. 510 (April – June 1971), 153-154.

1. Gospel sharing in every phase of life

2. Pulpit message and invitation

3. Priest involvement with Rhode Island group of leaders

4. Food pantries, community gardens

5. Kids program, nursing home ministry

Regarding techniques that the interviewees considered appropriate for NT evangelism from their *own* perspective, they noted:

1. Gospel sharing in every phase of life

2. Be Spirit-filled and get to know the other person

3. Prison ministry

4. Personal sharing

Survey Questions for Evangelism

How is personal communication established? The believer should show grace to the recipient by not only asking questions, but responding gracefully to their answers. Jerram Barrs suggested a method whereby the recipient is commended for their responses to opening questions.[302] Sometimes it is helpful to first find out if the recipient is ready

for a conversation. Some probing questions could be the following:[303]

1. What is your religious heritage?

2. Has your heritage helped you answer the important questions you are asking
   in life?

3. What are the questions you are asking?

Here is a list of survey questions:[304]

1. Do you believe in God?

2. Do you read the Bible?

3. Do you live in obedience to God's Laws?

4. Do you admire Christ?

5. Do you believe in afterlife and judgment?

D. James Kennedy offered this question for the recipient: "Do you know for sure that you

have eternal life?"[305]

---

[302] Jerram Barrs, *The Heart of Evangelism* (Wheaton, IL: Crossway Books, 2011), 207.

[303] Ken Hemphill, *Life Answers: Making Sense of Your World* (Nashville, TN: Lifeway Press, 1992), 13.

[304] Ibid.

[305] Kennedy, *Evangelism Explosion*, 15.

Applications of Findings

The summary of the research findings from the previous section developed an objective biblical and literary viewpoint of evangelism. This viewpoint is now used to either substantiate or disprove the hypotheses made by this author. As a precursor to this discussion, it should be noted that evangelism is a spiritually dynamic phenomenon. Figure 4 shows the spiritual relationships that are active prior to, during, and after the evangelistic event.[306] This figure depicts that there is a spiritual connection between the Holy Spirit and both the believer and the recipient as noted by the apostle Paul: "For it is by grace you are saved, through faith – and this is not from yourselves, it is the gift of God" (Ephesians 2:8-9). The link between the Holy Spirit and God's Word is confirmed in Hebrews 4:12: "For the word of God is alive and active. Sharper than any double-edged sword, it penetrates even to dividing soul and spirit, joints and marrow; it judges the thoughts and attitudes of the heart." The cross is displayed because it references the fact that Jesus Christ is the Word (John 1:14). Therefore, there is a divine governance that is present during the evangelistic encounter between the believer and the recipient, as noted from Ephesians 2. This is an important preface to this section, since an objective biblical and literary viewpoint is used to either substantiate or disprove the claims made by this author, but this viewpoint must hold true to Figure 4.

---

[306] Figure 4 is an adaptation (God's Word added to the figure) from James C. Logan, *Theology and Evangelism in the Wesleyan Heritage* (Nashville, TN: Abingdon Press, 1994), 54.

Holy

Spirit

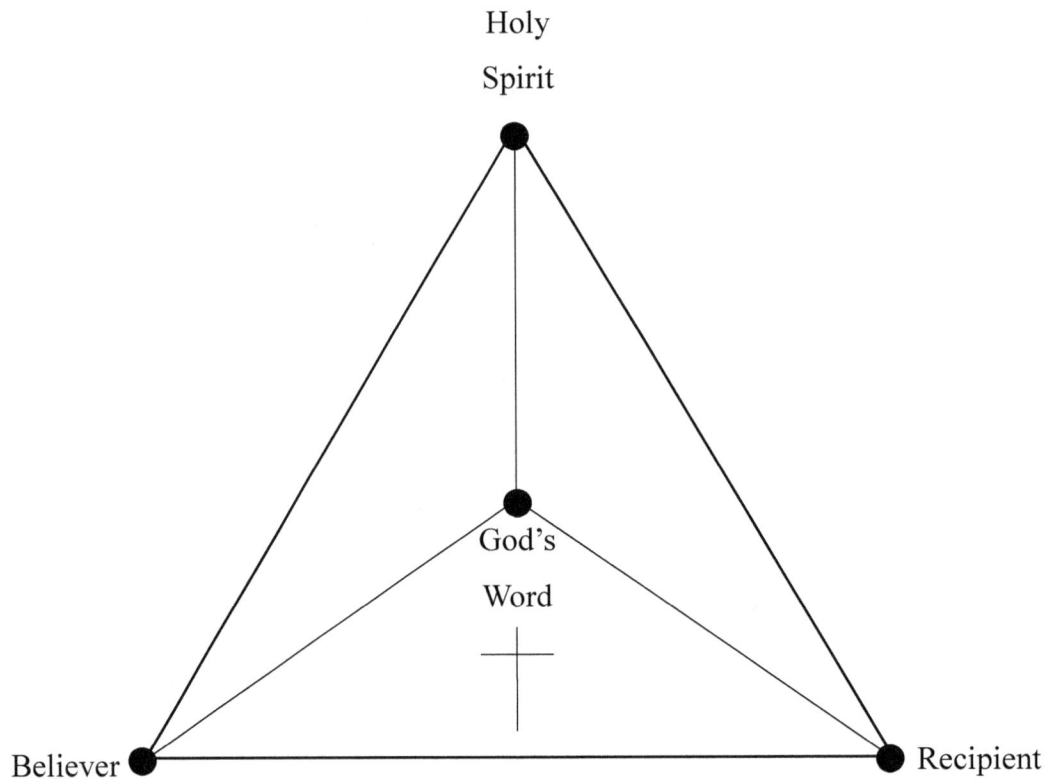

Figure 4. Spiritual relationships during evangelism

Hypothesis: Churches in Southeastern Massachusetts and Rhode Island are not

following the biblical mandate for evangelism.

The earlier section on Implications of Findings defined NT evangelism as the

sharing of the good news about Jesus Christ. However, only two of the interviewees

responded with a similar definition based on Matthew 5 and 28. This means that three out

of the five interviewees are not following the biblical mandate. This response ratio, 3/5,

or 0.6 exceeds the significance factor of 0.2 given in the Instrumentation section in

Chapter 3. Therefore, this phenomenon is statistically significant and rejects the null hypothesis (that the observed samples occurred by chance). This substantiates the claim made by this author that churches in Southeastern Massachusetts and Rhode Island are not following the biblical mandate for evangelism.

From the Church's viewpoint, the account in Luke 10:1-24 describes the commissioning of seventy-two believers to go out into "every town and place where he [Jesus] was about to go" (verse 1). The main focus is not whether this is personal evangelism, door-to-door evangelism, or world evangelism, but rather, the focus is on the "harvest" or need itself. In verse 2, Jesus explained that "The harvest is plentiful, but the workers are few. Ask the Lord of the harvest, therefore, to send out workers into his harvest field." Here we see the unique need of sharing Christ from God's point of view. Which point of view does the Church take today – Christ's or their own?

In contrast, all five interviewees indicated that their respective denominations do hold to a specific view regarding evangelism. The denominational views as indicated by the interviewees from the interview process (Table 10) varied greatly regarding evangelism:

1. Great Commission and church planting

2. Sending out two believers by the Missions committee

3. Sharing the love and news of Christ

4. Street evangelism and household Bible studies

5. Living the life of the gospel

Luke 10 indicates a need to send out workers into the harvest field. Some of the responses from the interviewees above indicate a similar task. But church planting and living the life of the gospel do not appear to fall under this category. Church planting, as genuine as it sounds, is not an active process of sharing the good news. Living the life of the gospel is admirable, but it does not in itself describe the sharing of the good news of Christ. Household Bible studies could be evangelistic, but they are traditionally comprised of believers rather than unbelievers. Therefore, out of the sample size of seven responses (church planting and household Bible studies are additional responses), the response ratio for those interviewees (church denominations) not following the biblical mandate is 3/7, or 0.43. This too, exceeds the significance factor of 0.2, *substantiating the claim that churches in Southeastern Massachusetts and Rhode Island are not following the biblical mandate for evangelism.* When asked if their respective denomination thinks that evangelism is important, two out of the five interviewees indicated that they thought their denomination did not think that evangelism is important. The response ratio for this is 0.4, which is consistent with the ratio of 0.43 noted above.

The point of view that members of these denominations have must be considered. The interviewees indicated that their fellow members have the following obstacles about sharing Christ:

1. Sharing the gospel is too difficult

2. They have a fear of other people

3. They are too comfortable in their church

When asked what their church could do to increase church awareness regarding evangelism in the local neighborhood, most of the interviewees responded with preaching from the pulpit. One interviewee suggested block parties and using the food program to increase awareness.

To help alleviate these concerns, a proper perspective of the Church regarding evangelism needs to be considered. The missional work for the local church is to "create a community of Kingdom people."[307] If we reference Matthew 28 which specifies the making of disciples, we must assert that this process of making disciples begins with a conversion of the heart. The conversion of the heart, however, is based on the sharing of the gospel, or evangelism. The Kingdom perspective, therefore, is for the local church to be effective in evangelism in order to provide the gospel message.

One method of incorporating evangelism is to have an evangelistic group within the local church focused on outreach.[308] This group would not only operate in obedience to God's Word, but would operate in a pragmatic fashion: "Let the ardent Christians form missionary groups of evangelistic bands that will meet once a week or once a month to make sure that 'our congregation does win the lost in our community and give birth to daughter congregations at home and abroad.'"[309] Thus, the incorporation of evangelism leads to Church growth. This is not just necessarily a constant monitoring of numbers of

---

[307] Ben Campbell Johnson, *Rethinking Evangelism* (Philadelphia, PA: The Westminster Press, 1987), 121.
[308] McGavran, *Effective Evangelism,* 46.
[309] Ibid.

believers in each congregation, but a realization that the overall Church is growing according to Christ's plan.

Hypothesis: Most churches in Southeastern Massachusetts and Rhode Island do not understand the theology of New Testament evangelism.

From Ephesians 4:11, the word "evangelists" (*euangelistes*) means the "one who declares good news."[310] From Table 9, four of the five interviewees indicated that evangelism involves speaking to others outside of the church body about Christ (including references to the Great Commission in Matthew 28). The fifth interviewee considered evangelism as "teaching Christian values." This is outside of the bounds of the Scriptural definition. Since one interviewee did not recognize evangelism as speaking to others, this results in a response ratio of 0.2 which is equal to the significance factor. Since the response ratio is not greater than the significance factor we cannot reject the null hypothesis, therefore this result occurred by chance. Since the majority of the interviewees indicated that evangelism involves speaking to others outside of the church body about Christ, *we must reject the author's hypothesis that most churches in Southeastern Massachusetts and Rhode Island do not understand New Testament evangelism.*

Two of the interviewees from the interview process made explicit reference to Matthew 5 (being salt and light) and Matthew 28 (the Great Commission). Another

---

[310] Zodhiates and Baker, *Hebrew-Greek Key Word Study Bible,* 1628.

interviewee made reference to the conversation between Jesus and the Samaritan woman in John 4. Still another interviewee, in commenting about the sharing of the gospel, referenced 1 Corinthians 1:18 which mentions that the message of the cross is the power of God.

Hypothesis: The cultural setting for churches today in Southeastern Massachusetts and Rhode Island is vastly different than that of the Middle East 2000 years ago.

The geographical scope of evangelism is everywhere.[311] Therefore, there are no limitations as to where the gospel can be spread; this could be the local neighborhood, the city, the country, as well as other countries. Jesus was specific about this when He said, "But you will receive power when the Holy Spirit comes on you; and you will be my witnesses in Jerusalem, and in all Judea and Samaria, and to the ends of the earth" (Acts 1:8).

We note, however, that Acts 8:1-3 describes the cultural setting in the Middle East where the recipients were not receptive to the gospel:

> On that day a great persecution broke out against the church in Jerusalem, and all except the apostles were scattered throughout Judea and Samaria. Godly men buried Stephen and mourned deeply for him. But Saul began to destroy the church. Going from house to house, he dragged off both men and women and put them in prison.

---

[311] Huston, *Crusade Evangelism and the Local Church,* 35.

We can say that evangelism was practiced, because men and women were put into prison. It was publicly known because Saul was aware of who was practicing their Christian faith.

The cultural setting for churches today in Southeastern Massachusetts and Rhode Island is similar. From Table 8, we note that all five interviewees thought that their immediate neighborhood was not responsive to evangelism. The response ratio here is 1.0, which is well above the significance factor of 0.2. Therefore, we can reject the null hypothesis (these responses did not occur by chance). Since the evidence is similar for the two cultural settings, *we must reject the author's hypothesis that the cultural setting for churches today in Southeastern Massachusetts and Rhode Island is vastly different than that of the Middle East 2000 years ago.*

Believers should prepare for evangelism by understanding how recipients feel about the gospel. From Table 11, the reasons why they perceived that these people are not responsive are:

1. They have a negative view of the Church and Christianity

2. They are caught up in the world

3. They are too comfortable

4. They have existing presuppositions about spiritual things

The interviewees also provided what they considered as the major obstacles that the local residents have towards accepting Christ:

1. They do not want to change

2. They do not see the need

3. Sin

4. Our regions is the least biblically-literate

Despite these obstacles, believers can engage in a conversation with a recipient by asking them if they believe in spiritual things. They can also ask them if they would be willing to take a survey. The "How Good Are You" tract (www.ProclaimCourse.com) shows a scale from one to ten regarding a person's "goodness." The believer could then ask the recipient how they rate themselves on the scale. Most recipients rate themselves less than a ten. They are then asked if they have ever broken one of the listed Ten Commandments. They are typically honest and admit they have broken at least one commandment. The believer then continues that the result of sin is eternal death and that Christ died for our sins, resulting in eternal life for those who confess their sin and ask Him for forgiveness. They are then invited to pray with the believer for forgiveness.

Research Question: What are the similarities and differences between churches in Southeastern Massachusetts and Rhode Island and the evangelism as practiced in the New Testament by Jesus Christ, His disciples, and the apostle Paul, and how can churches in Southeastern Massachusetts and Rhode Island focus more on New Testament evangelism?

To address the similarities and differences, we initially turn to whether or not most churches in Southeastern Massachusetts and Rhode Island understand the theology of New Testament evangelism. We noted earlier in this chapter that, based on the evidence provided, we rejected this author's hypothesis that these churches do not understand the theology of NT evangelism. This is a good foundation for the churches to have, since evangelism cannot be practiced until it is adequately understood.

We also noted, however, that the hypothesis that churches in Southeastern Massachusetts and Rhode Island are not following the biblical mandate for evangelism is true based on the evidence provided. This leads us to the fact that more can be done today by these churches. There is a spiritual void in these churches, since the biblical mandate to perform evangelism is not adequately realized. The underlying thrust of this dissertation is to realize that a gap exists in this area. This is an important realization, because action cannot be taken until these churches realize this.

We rejected the author's hypothesis based on the evidence given that the cultural setting for churches today in Southeastern Massachusetts and Rhode Island is vastly different than that of the Middle East 2000 years ago. The climate, as noted earlier in this chapter, is the same between the two settings. The same obstacles exist between the two settings. Numerous suggestions have been provided in Chapters 2 and 4 to help churches in Southeastern Massachusetts and Rhode Island to focus more on New Testament evangelism. Are these churches willing to respond?

Further Study

The thrust of the exegesis was to answer the following questions which were reformatted from the hypotheses stated earlier:

1. What is the theology of NT evangelism?

2. What is the biblical mandate for NT evangelism?

3. What is the cultural setting for NT evangelism?

The exegesis given in Chapter 2 was not intended to be a thorough interpretation of Scripture based on the topic of evangelism. That task could be taken on as further study.

In addition, literary presuppositions from various authors were analyzed and critiqued objectively in Chapter 2. These presuppositions were developed to answer the three questions listed above. They focused on perspectives from various authors – some having commonality and some appearing perhaps contradictory. These presuppositions were not intended to be a thorough analysis and critique on evangelism. That task could be taken on as further study.

There are 648 churches in Rhode Island[312] and 857 churches in Southeastern Massachusetts as of this writing.[313] It would be a difficult endeavor timewise to interview

---

[312] "Yellow Pages," Yahoo, accessed February 18, 2016, http://www.yellowpages.com/providence-ri/churches.

[313] "Yellow Pages," Yahoo, accessed February 18, 2016, http://www.yellowpages.com/search?search_terms=churches&geo_location_terms=Rehoboth%2C+MA.

a biblical leader from each one of these churches. Perhaps this could be considered as a further study. Even within the Christian realm, there are numerous denominations and this research is not intended to analyze all of them. An analysis of all denominations (as well as the churches within these denominations) would be too exhaustive for this research, but could be continued as a further study beyond this research.

Furthermore, the portion of the research question dealing with how churches in these areas can be more focused on evangelism did not result in a comprehensive list of improvements. Such a list may be too comprehensive for any dissertation or publication. An additional list of improvements for churches in these areas could be continued as a further study.

Appendix A

Interview Questions

1. How would you define New Testament evangelism?

2. What techniques do *you* think are appropriate for New Testament evangelism?

3. Does your denomination hold to any specific views regarding evangelism?

4. Does your denomination think that evangelism is important?

5. What techniques does your *denomination* deem appropriate for New Testament evangelism?

6. Which New Testament Scriptures do you think are applicable to evangelism?

7. What techniques on evangelism do you see as being applied in the New Testament?

8. Do you think that your immediate neighborhood is responsive to evangelism? Why or why not?

9. What do you think are the major obstacles that local residents have in regards to accepting Christ?

10. What do you think are the major obstacles that your fellow church members have in regards to sharing Christ?

11. What do you think your church can do to increase church awareness regarding evangelism in the local neighborhood?

Appendix B

Responses to Interview Questions

Southern Baptist

1. How would you define New Testament evangelism?

    The basis is the Great Commission – both individual & corporate. There is a two-fold purpose: conversion and discipleship. This must be propagated all the way through to multiplication. For the corporate church, all activities must have conversion and discipleship in mind.

2. What techniques do *you* think are appropriate for New Testament evangelism?

    There is no real technique - just be prepared to share gospel in each phase of daily life. Even the mundane, ordinary opportunities may be God-ordained.

3. Does your denomination hold to any specific views regarding evangelism?

    Evangelism is a mandate from God's Word (Great Commission). However, they also emphasize church planting based on the apostle Paul.

4. Does your denomination think that evangelism is important?

    Yes. Baptists spend millions of dollars on evangelism. If a church plant sends a proposal for an outreach event, then the Baptist Convention will pay for the event.

5. What techniques does your *denomination* deem appropriate for New Testament evangelism?

Same as #2.

6. Which New Testament Scriptures do you think are applicable to evangelism?

    Matthew 28:18-20; Romans 3:23, 6:23, 5:8, 10:11-12; John 14:6, 3:16; Acts 4:12;

    Matthew 5; Revelation 20:11-15.

7. What techniques on evangelism do you see as being applied in the New Testament?

    Some examples are: the Samaritan woman at the well John 4 (across cross-cultural

    lines), Paul doing street preaching in Acts 17 at Athens (Acropolis), Paul in the

    synagogues; Paul and Silas doing street-preaching at Philippi, and Jesus engaged with

    the people (e.g. Pharisees).

8. Do you think that your immediate neighborhood is responsive to evangelism? Why or

    why not?

    No. Society is hardened to gospel and has negative view of Church and Christianity.

    This is true the majority of the time.

9. What do you think are the major obstacles that local residents have in regards to

    accepting Christ?

    Many residents feel that affiliation with a local church is sufficient for salvation.

    Also, family influence interferes with a person's opportunity to accept Christ. Barna

    research shows that our region of the country is the least biblically-literate.

10. What do you think are the major obstacles that your fellow church members have in

    regards to sharing Christ?

New Testament Evangelism

Fear of rejection, personal perception that sharing the gospel is difficult, concern about interference from other religions, and failure to see the process of "sharing the gospel through the lens of eternity."

11. What do you think your church can do to increase church awareness regarding evangelism in the local neighborhood?

Keep talking about it (both corporately and individually). It is not just a concept, it is a mandate. Remind them of what Christ has done for them and the reality of the Great White Throne seat of judgment.

Independent Fundamental Baptist

1. How would you define New Testament evangelism?

   The fulfillment of Christ and His commission to the Church in Mathew 28 and Mark 16. It is the good news and essence of why Christ came.

2. What techniques do *you* think are appropriate for New Testament evangelism?

   One needs to be Spirit-filled before soul-winning and must be willing to share with anyone. They must get to know a person's likes and dislikes and show personal care for the other person (i.e. talk about daily life of the other person). They should also look for concerns and consider how to approach the other person with the gospel. They must look for an opportunity to interject the gospel into the conversation. They should look for non-threatening dialogue to share Jesus with that person in order to earn their trust.

3. Does your denomination hold to any specific views regarding evangelism?

   Everything should be accomplished through the local church (e.g. the missions committee prays and considers needs). Men must be raised up to fulfill the mission in either the local church or the seminary. People should be sent out as a team two-by-two and must be accountable to the local church. They must be sent out to a people, not a place. Note that Paul was an apostle to the Gentiles and Peter to the Jews. One must follow the Spirit's leading as to where and how to go.

4. Does your denomination think that evangelism is important?

No.

5. What techniques does your *denomination* deem appropriate for New Testament evangelism?

Baptists preach from the pulpit and extend an invitation at the end of the message.

6. Which New Testament Scriptures do you think are applicable to evangelism?

John 3 (the entire chapter – Nicodemus you must be born again); John 4 (the Samaritan woman); 2 Timothy 4; Acts 1:8; Hebrews 10:3, 10:23; Isaiah 53.

7. What techniques on evangelism do you see as being applied in the New Testament?

Mathew 10 indicates that Jesus sent the disciples out two-by-two. Paul believed it was a personal sharing (that is what he experienced on the road to Damascus).

8. Do you think that your immediate neighborhood is responsive to evangelism? Why or why not?

No. They are mostly caught up in the world.

9. What do you think are the major obstacles that local residents have in regards to accepting Christ?

They have a misconception of who Christ is and what salvation is all about. They think that it is by works to get salvation.

10. What do you think are the major obstacles that your fellow church members have in regards to sharing Christ?

"God has not called me to be an evangelist." They just don't want to do it because it
is a hard thing to do.

11. What do you think your church can do to increase church awareness regarding
evangelism in the local neighborhood?

Preach from the pulpit to perform that local evangelism needs to be performed.

People need to be excited about sharing Christ with others and educate or train them.

Encourage Scripture memory to assist them in sharing.

Greek Orthodox

1. How would you define New Testament evangelism?

    Teaching values and faith in Christianity including faith in God and treating other

    people accordingly.

2. What techniques do *you* think are appropriate for New Testament evangelism?

    One could have an open discussion with prisoners including lessons in Bible stories.

    Prisoners would then discuss the application. This is a group conversation – let the

    prisoners talk and allow them to express themselves (i.e. listen to them).

3. Does your denomination hold to any specific views regarding evangelism?

    We are called to share the love and good news of Jesus Christ with people (which

    may not include conversion), with the intention of forming a personal relationship

    with Christ.

4. Does your denomination think that evangelism is important?

    Yes. It is about proclaiming truth and acting in a loving manner.

5. What techniques does your *denomination* deem appropriate for New Testament

    evangelism?

    The priest is involved with a RI group of leaders. Also, the denomination prescribes

    Communion, daily prayer, and frequent attendance at worship.

6. Which New Testament Scriptures do you think are applicable to evangelism?

Matthew 25 is important for the prisoners in terms of meeting other people. It gives

prisoners a better idea how to lead their lives with respect to God when they are

released.

7. What techniques on evangelism do you see as being applied in the New Testament?

The teachings from Christ as well as the writers of the epistles in regard to Jesus

Christ.

8. Do you think that your immediate neighborhood is responsive to evangelism? Why or

why not?

No. People are set in their ways with existing presuppositions or have a church they

are going to. Most people would be uncomfortable with somebody coming to the

door.

9. What do you think are the major obstacles that local residents have in regards to

accepting Christ?

People do not see a need or are not interested.

10. What do you think are the major obstacles that your fellow church members have in

regards to sharing Christ?

Fear of other people. Also, the focus within a parish is on doing existing tasks.

Changing or doing something knew would be difficult due to being set in their ways

(i.e. certain presuppositions). New people are either born into or married into the

parish, since some portions of the service are spoken in Greek.

11. What do you think your church can do to increase church awareness regarding

evangelism in the local neighborhood?

Articulating similarities and differences of orthodoxy (Greek) with other people.

Greek Orthodox is neither Catholic nor Protestant. It has probably 300 million

members.

Methodist

1. How would you define New Testament evangelism?

    Acts 26:16-18.

2. What techniques do *you* think are appropriate for New Testament evangelism?

    One on one: a believer approaching the recipient (i.e. a friend), soap box preaching (although it is questionable as to whether it is effective), small groups (invited by a friend to a household Bible study), Holy clubs started by John & Charles Wesley which are similar to household Bible study, neighborhood outreach by meeting new neighbors and inviting them to church (although not much of this is happening), electronic media, online devotionals, and the training of pastors.

3. Does your denomination hold to any specific views regarding evangelism?
    Methodism started very strong in evangelism in the mid-1800s with the Holy club as mentioned above. John and Charles Wesley wrote hymns, and performed street evangelism.

4. Does your denomination think that evangelism is important?

    For today, not as important as it used to be.

5. What techniques does your *denomination* deem appropriate for New Testament evangelism?
    Need-based opportunities (without a gospel presentation): food pantries, community gardens, missionary trips to needy areas. Also, the United Methodist Commission on Relief is one of first sources of relief in the world.

6. Which New Testament Scriptures do you think are applicable to evangelism?

   Use these verses to lead someone to Christ:

   - Romans 8:1 – no condemnation for those who are in Christ

   - 1 Corinthians 1:18 – preaching of the cross is to them that perish foolishness, but unto us which are saved it is the power of God.

   - 1 Corinthians 2:6 – we speak the wisdom of God but not the wisdom of this age.

   - 1 Timothy 4:11-13 – these things command and teach. Let no man despise thy youth but be an example of the believers, in Word, in conversation, in charity, in spirit, in faith, in purity.

7. What techniques on evangelism do you see as being applied in the New Testament?

   The sharing of resources (the Bereans considered this as part of the gospel), healing in many instances, and preaching in Acts 26

8. Do you think that your immediate neighborhood is responsive to evangelism? Why or why not?

   No. We were involved in a neighborhood Bible study for many years. I don't know how receptive our area would be to an evangelistic outreach.

9. What do you think are the major obstacles that local residents have in regards to accepting Christ?

   Sin (blocks the gospel presentation), traditional thinking, and pre-conceived spiritual beliefs.

10. What do you think are the major obstacles that your fellow church members have in regards to sharing Christ?

They have a strong reluctance to change from not-sharing to sharing Christ (i.e. right now people are comfortable and would not consider sharing Christ). It is very difficult to make a change in the existing local church culture. Believers are comfortable concerning knowing about Christ but not sharing Him.

11. What do you think your church can do to increase church awareness regarding evangelism in the local neighborhood?

Increase the budget for local evangelism, assign small groups for specific purposes (e.g. food pantry, door-to-door visitation), provide direction to small group leaders regarding evangelism and invite them to consider specific gifts of certain people to meet mission needs.

Non-Denominational

1. How would you define New Testament evangelism?

    Spreading the gospel of Jesus Christ: He died on the cross for us and by His blood we
    are saved (for those who believe in Him). Believers are to be a light to others.

2. What techniques do *you* think are appropriate for New Testament evangelism?

    Getting to know the recipient and understand where they are at, answering questions
    in the work place using Scripture, and door-to-door visitations.

3. Does your denomination hold to any specific views regarding evangelism?

    A believer must live a life based on the gospel to be effective.

4. Does your denomination think that evangelism is important?

    Yes.

5. What techniques does your *denomination* deem appropriate for New Testament
    evangelism?

    Kids program, nursing home ministry, world missions, sending out young adults to
    the mission field (one or two weeks at a time), involvement with Wycliffe Bible
    translators, and the food program including the sharing of the gospel and praying for
    them.

6. Which New Testament Scriptures do you think are applicable to evangelism?

    – Acts 13:47 - salvation to the ends of the earth

    – Mark 16:15 - preaching the gospel

New Testament Evangelism

- Acts 20:24 - defining the good news of God's grace

- Matthew 5:15-16 - let your light shine

- Romans 1:16 - not ashamed of the gospel

- 1 Peter 3:15 - be able to give an answer

- Matthew 5:14 - share the light of world

- Matthew 28:19-20 – the Great Commission

- 1 Corinthians 15:1-2 – by the gospel you are saved

- Romans 10:17 - faith comes from hearing the message

- Mark 8:35 - but whoever loses their life for my sake will save it

- Titus 2:1 - keep sound doctrine

- John 13:35 - you are my disciples if love one another

- Acts 1:8 - witnesses in Jerusalem

- 1 Corinthians 2:2 - I know nothing among you but Christ crucified.

7. What techniques on evangelism do you see as being applied in the New Testament?

One has to be bold in the Holy Spirit and not be ashamed of it and go out into the world and preach the gospel.

8. Do you think that your immediate neighborhood is responsive to evangelism? Why or why not?

No. Everybody is comfortable with their cars and lives. They don't want to get out of their comfort zone ("I'm ok and I'm going to heaven"). Also, they consider Christians that go around preaching weird.

New Testament Evangelism

9. What do you think are the major obstacles that local residents have in regards to accepting Christ?

They don't want to change their life because they are doing ok. They would be concerned about making a major change because they may have to give up something.

10. What do you think are the major obstacles that your fellow church members have in regards to sharing Christ?

They are too comfortable in the local church. They are settled into their comfort zone after years. They don't want to shake things up. They are afraid they don't know Scripture enough and are not trained in spreading the gospel. Therefore, they don't feel adequate and don't want to be made fun of.

11. What do you think your church can do to increase church awareness regarding evangelism in the local neighborhood?

They can schedule a block party with a table with information and have games for the kids. They can knock on doors and invite people for the Resurrection Day service. They can use the food program to increase awareness.

Bibliography

Abraham, William J. *The Logic of Evangelism.* Grand Rapids, MI: William B. Eerdmans Publishing Company, 1989.

Aldrich, Joseph C. *Lifestyle Evangelism: Crossing Traditional Barriers to Reach the Unbelieving World.* Portland, OR: Multnomah Press, 1978.

Aria, Mortimer and Alan Johnson. *The Great Commission: Biblical Models for Evangelism.* Nashville, TN: Abingdon Press, 1992.

Armstrong, Richard Stoll. *Service Evangelism.* Philadelphia, PA: The Westminster Press, 1979.

Autrey, C.E. *Evangelism in the Acts.* Grand Rapids, MI: Zondervan, 1964.

Barna, George. *Generation Next.* Ventura, CA: Regal, 1995.

Barrs, Jerram. *The Heart of Evangelism.* Wheaton, IL: Crossway Books, 2011.

Beougher, Timothy and Alvin Reid, eds. *Evangelism for a Changing World.* Wheaton, IL: Harold Shaw Publishers, 1995.

Bock, Darrell L. and Mike Del Rosario. "The Table Briefing: Tone and Truth in Cultural Engagement." *Bibliotheca Sacra* 173 (January – March, 2016): 99-106.

Bounds, E.M. *Power through Prayer.* Springdale, PA: Whitaker House, 1982.

Braaten, Carl E. *"The Meaning of Evangelism in the Context of God's Universal Grace."* In *The Story of Evangelism: Exploring a Missional Practice of the Church.* edited by Paul W. Chilcote and Laceye C. Warner, 162-163. Grand Rapids, MI: William B. Eerdmans Publishing Company, 2008.

Brown, Calvin. ed. *New International Dictionary of New Testament Theology.* Grand Rapids, MI: Zondervan Publishing House, 1976.

Bruns, Roger A. *Preacher: Billy Sunday & Big-Time American Evangelism.* New York, NY: W.W. Norton & Company, 1992.

Carson, D.A. *The Gagging of God: Christianity Confronts Pluralism.* Grand Rapids, MI: Zondervan Publishing House, 1996.

New Testament Evangelism

Cassidy, Michael. "The Third Way." *International Review of Mission* 63, no.249 (1974): 9-23.

Cecil, Douglas M. Review of Bailey E. Smith. *Real Evangelism.* Nashville, TN: Word Publishing, 1999. *Bibliotheca Sacra* 157, no. 628 (October – December 2000): 505.

Chia, Poh Fang. "Doesn't God Care?" *Our Daily Bread* 60, no. 6 (June 2015), 1-30.

_____. "Gentle Lights." *Our Daily Bread* 60, no. 8 (August 2015): 1-31.

Chilcote, Paul W. and Laceye C. Warner, eds. *The Study of Evangelism: Exploring a Missional Practice of the Church.* Grand Rapids, MI: William B. Eerdmans Publishing Company, 2008.

Coleman, Robert E. *Evangelism in Perspective.* Harrisburg, PA: Christian Publications, Inc., 1975.

_____. *The Master Plan of Evangelism.* Grand Rapids, MI: Fleming H. Revell, 1993.

_____. *The Master's Way of Personal Evangelism.* Wheaton, IL: Crossway Books, 1997.

Dawn, Marva J. *Reaching Out without Dumbing Down: A Theology of Worship for this Urgent Time.* Grand Rapids, MI: Eerdmans Publishing Company, 1995.

Dayton, Edward R. and David A. Frazier. *Planning Strategies for World Evangelization.* Grand Rapids, MI: William B. Eerdmans Publishing Company, 1990.

Dobbins, Gaines. *Evangelism According to Christ.* Nashville, TN: Broadman, 1949.

Douglas, J.D., ed. *Let the Earth Hear His Voice.* Minneapolis, MN: World Wide Publications, 1975.

Finney, John. *Emerging Evangelism.* London: Darton, Longman and Todd Ltd, 2004.

Fish, Roy J. and J.B. Conant. *Every Member Evangelism for Today.* New York, NY: Harper and Row Publishers, 1922.

Freeman, James M. *Manners and Customs of the Bible.* Plainfield, NJ: Logos International, 1972.

Getz, G.A. Review of *Saturation Evangelism*. George W. Peters. *Bibliotheca Sacra* 128, no 510 (April – June 1971): 153-154.

Graham, Billy. "Why Lausanne." Keynote address, Palais de Beaulieu, Lausanne, Switzerland, July 16, 1974.

Green, Michael. *Evangelism in the Early Church*. Grand Rapids, MI: Eerdmans, 1970.

_____. *Evangelism through the Local Church*. Nashville, TN: Thomas Nelson Publishers, 1990.

Hemphill, Ken. *Life Answers: Making Sense of Your World*. Nashville, TN: Lifeway Press, 1992.

Hunter III, George G. "The Apostolic Identity of the Church and Wesleyan Christianity." In *Theology and Evangelism in the Wesleyan Heritage,* edited by James C. Logan, 169. Nashville, TN: Abingdon Press, 1994.

_____. *The Contagious Congregation: Frontiers on Evangelism and Church Growth*. Nashville, TN: Abingdon Press, 1979.

Huston, Sterling W. *Crusade Evangelism and the Local Church*. Minneapolis, MN: World Wide Publications, 1984.

Johnson, Ben. *Evangelism Primer*. Atlanta, GA: John Knox Press, 1983.

_____. *Rethinking Evangelism*. Philadelphia, PA: The Westminster Press, 1987.

Keck, Leander E. *The Church Confident*. Nashville, TN: Abingdon Press, 1993.

Kennedy, D. James. *Evangelism Explosion*. London: Coverdale House Publishers, 1970.

Lagasse, Paul. *Understanding All About God: How to Obtain Eternal Life*. Accessed February 29, 2016. http://understandingallaboutgod.com.

Logan, James C. *Theology and Evangelism in the Wesleyan Heritage*. Nashville, TN: Abingdon Press, 1994.

Lutzer, Erwin W. *Hitler's Cross*. Chicago, IL: Moody Press, 1995.

Matthews, C.E. *The Southern Baptist Program of Evangelism*. Atlanta, GA: Home Mission Board, 1949.

McCloskey, Mark. *Tell it Often – Tell it Well.* San Bernardino, CA: Here's Life
        Publishers, 1985.

McDow, Malcolm and Alvin Reid. *Firefall: How God has Shaped History through
        Revivals.* Nashville, TN: Broadman & Holman Publishers, 1997.

McGavran, Donald A. *Effective Evangelism: A Theological Mandate.* Phillipsburg, NJ:
        Presbyterian & Reformed Publishing Company, 1988.

McLoughlin, William G. *Modern Revivalism.* New York, NY: Ronald Press, 1959.

Merriam, Sharan B. and Edwin L. Simpson. *A Guide to Research for Educators and
        Trainers of Adults.* 2nd ed. Malabar, FL: Krieger Publishing Company, 2000.

Moberg, David O. *The Great Reversal: Evangelism and Social Concern.* Rev. ed.
        Philadelphia, PA: J.B. Lippincott Company, 1977.

Moyers, Bill. "America's Religious Mosaic." *USA Weekend* (11-13 October 1996): 5.

Mueller, Walt. *Understanding Today's Youth Culture.* Wheaton, IL: Tyndale, 1994.

Nichols, Bruce J. ed. *In Word and Deed: Evangelism and Social Responsibility.* Grand
        Rapids, MI: William B. Eerdmans Publishing Company, 1985.

Peterson, Jim. *Evangelism as a Lifestyle.* Colorado Springs, CO: NavPress, 1980.

Pfeiffer, Charles F. and Everett F. Harrison, eds. *The Wycliffe Bible Commentary.*
        Chicago, IL: Moody Press, 1962.

Rainer, Thom S. *The Bridger Generation.* Nashville, TN: Broadman & Holman
        Publishers, 1997.

Ratz, Calvin, Frank Tillapaugh, and Myron Ausburger. *Mastering Outreach &
        Evangelism.* Portland, OR: Multnomah, 1990.

Rein, Kristen. *USA College Today.* Last modified January 5, 2016. Accessed March 14,
        2016. http://college.usatoday.com/2016/01/05/survey-millenials-views-of-
        religion-news-media-grows-increasingly-negative.

Robinson, Darrell W. *People Sharing Jesus.* Nashville, TN: Thomas Nelson Publishers,
        1995.

Roper, David. "The Two Bears." *Our Daily Bread* 60, no. 8 (August 2015): 1-31.

Runyon, Ronald D. "Principles and Methods of Household Evangelism." *Bibliotheca Sacra* 142, no. 565 (January-March 1985): 64-74.

Sanders, J. Oswald, *Spiritual Leadership: Principles of Excellence for Every Believer.* Chicago, IL: Moody Press, 1994.

Sider, Ronald J. "Evangelism, Salvation and Social Justice: Definitions and Interrelationships." *International Review of Mission* 64, no. 255 (July 1975): 251-257.

Stott, John. *Christian Mission in the Modern World.* Downers Grove, IL: InterVarsity Press, 1975.

_____. *The Lausanne Covenant: An Exposition and Commentary.* Minneapolis, MN: World Wide Publications, 1975.

_____. "The Nature of Biblical Evangelism." Lecture, Palais de Beaulieu, Lausanne, Switzerland, July 16, 1974.

Taylor, J.V. *Change of Address.* London: Hodder & Stoughton, 1968.

Tyson, Joseph B. *The New Testament and Early Christianity.* New York, NY: MacMillan Publishing Company, 1984.

VanHorn, Stephen. "*Oikos* Evangelism and Church Growth." M.A.B.S. Thesis, International Christian Graduate University, School of Theology, Arrowhead Springs, CA, 1981.

Wagner, C. Peter. *Strategies for Church Growth: Tools for Effective Mission and Evangelism.* Ventura, CA: Regal Books, 1987.

_____. *Your Church Can be Healthy.* Nashville, TN: Abingdon Press, 1979.

Walker, Alan. *The New Evangelism.* Nashville, TN: Abingdon Press, 1975.

Watson, David Lowes. "Evangelism: A Disciplinary Approach." *International Bulletin of Missionary Research* 7, no. 1 (January 1983): 6-9.

Webber, Robert E. *Liturgical Evangelism: Worship as Outreach and Nurture.* Harrisburg, PA: Morehouse Publishing, 1986.

White, James Emery. *Opening the Front Door: Worship and Church Growth.* Nashville, TN: Convention Press, 1992.

Whitney, Donald S. *Spiritual Disciplines for the Christian Life.* Colorado Springs, CO: NavPress, 1991.

Wimber, John and Kevin Springer. *Power Evangelism.* San Francisco, CA: Harper & Row Publishers, 1986.

Willard, Dallas. *The Spirit of the Disciplines: Understanding How God Changes Lives.* San Francisco, CA: Harper & Row Publishers, 1988.

"Yellow Pages." Yahoo, accessed February 18, 2016. http://www.yellowpages.com/providence-ri/churches.

"Yellow Pages." Yahoo, accessed February 18, 2016. http://www.yellowpages.com/search?search_terms=churches&geo_location_terms=Rehoboth%2C+MA.

Yoder, John. *The Politics of Jesus.* Grand Rapids, MI: William B. Eerdmans Publishing Company, 1972.

Zodhiates, Spiros and Warren Baker, eds. *Hebrew-Greek Key Word Study Bible: Key Insights into God's Word.* Chattanooga, TN: AMG Publishers, 1996.